At Home with God

Stories of Life, Love, and Laughter

By Sharon Jaynes

At Home with God
Stories of Life, Love, and Laughter
ISBN 1-58919-503-5

Published by RiverOak Publishing
P.O. Box 700143
Tulsa, Oklahoma 74170-0143

Illustrations by Elise Peterson

Dedication

This book is dedicated to the two special men in my life. One captivated my heart the first time our eyes met at a college Bible study in 1979 and the other the moment our eyes locked in the delivery room in 1984. Thank you, Steve, for being a godly husband who has loved me unconditionally and led our family into a deeper walk with the Lord. Thank you, Steven, for being such a wonderful son. You have been one of God's greatest blessings. He gave me everything I ever wanted in a child, wrapped up in one package, when He gave me you.

Acknowledgments

I would like to thank all of the friends who are mentioned in this book. My life has been enriched by knowing each one of you, and I count it a privilege to be able to share you with others and enrich their lives as well.

I am forever grateful to Lysa TerKeurst, my partner at The Proverbs 31 Ministry, who has been my cheerleader all the way. Without Lysa encouraging me forward and believing in me, these stories would still be hidden away in a drawer collecting dust.

I also want to thank my agent, Janet Kobobel Grant, for getting my "house" in order. She redesigned the floor plan, rearranged the furniture, and suggested the finishing touches.

A special thanks to my editor, Barbara Scott. I so appreciate her gentle spirit and sensitivity to God's leading.

A special thanks also goes to my husband, Steve, and my son, Steven, for enduring piles of papers and listening to all my stories.

Most of all, I thank the Lord for opening my eyes to see His presence in our home, for helping me sense His nudges in ordinary life situations, and for reaching down and drawing me to Himself.

Contents

Foreword 9

The Porch—*Welcome to All* 13
The Melting Pot 14
Masterpiece by the Bay 18
Potluck 21
It's What's on the Inside that Counts 26
Just Say No to Neighbors 30
Someone's Knocking 33
Prayer 36

The Kitchen—*Sustenance for Life* 39
How's Your Reception? 40
Confidence to Bank On 47
Led Astray 51
The Perm 56
Emergency! Emergency! 59
Let's Joust, Daddy! 61
No Clams for Larry 64
A Watched Pot Never Burns 66
Thank You, Lord, for My Dirty Floor 70
Reptiles and Rodents 72
Squawking or Chirping? 75
Which Character Will You Play? 78
Prayer 83

The Family Room—*Surrounded by Love* 85
Grandma's Inheritance 86
A Little Child Shall Lead Them 90
Dear Mommy 94
Putting on the Dog 98
Lassie Come Home 100
Nightmare on York Street 104
Who's the Boss? 109
From Diaper Cream to Acne Cream 112
The Gift 116
The Wonder of You: To Steven from Mom 120
Prayer 126

The Bedroom—*Rest for the Weary* 129
Mrs. Jaynes, You're Leading Again 130
Trick Skis 134
Be Still My Heart 137
Would You Be Afraid? 141
Collect Call 144

Bushwhacker 147
Dr. Snow White and the Seven Dwarfs 150
Lame Man Dancing....153
Prayer 158

The Bathroom—*Clean at Last* 161
The Auctioning Block 162
Three Squirrels....165
Beached 169
City Slickers 173
God's Speedometer 177
Into the Hands of Man 182
A Way of Escape....185
Disclosing Tablets 189
Under Construction....191
Prayer 195

The Hallway—*Moving On* 197
Guess Who I Bumped into Today?....198
Swollen Imaginations 201
The Bride in the Box 204
Rearview Driving 208
Hot Head, Cold Feet 211
Overheating—Again 213
Swine or Truth? 218
The Baby in the Nile 221
Circles in the Sand 225
Prayer 230

The Stairs—*Moving Up* 233
Grafted 234
Time Traveler 238
The Winner 240
The Right Credentials 244
The Interview....247
Messenger from Heaven 251
Inducted....254
The Guest Book....257
Paul's Return 261
An Easter Bride 264
Prayer 267

Conclusion—*At Home with God* 269

About the Author....271

Foreword

After a scattered day of errands, traffic, ball games, and meetings, I am on my way home at last. The car seems to steer itself like a faithful steed making its way to the stable. I turn into my neighborhood, round the final corner of my street, and there it sits—my house, snuggled in the darkness with one tiny light welcoming me home. A lone candle in the window reminds me that my refuge waits to nourish, comfort, and refresh my soul.

I'm sure that passersby have often wondered about my candle in the window. Is it perhaps an oversight, the forgotten remains of Christmas that was somehow overlooked when the decorations were being packed away? No, this tiny flicker is not a misplaced ornament but a daily reminder that this is a home where the Light of the world resides, speaks to its inhabitants, and welcomes all who walk through its doors.

God has always desired to be at home with His children. He strolled through the garden in the cool of the evening with Adam and Eve; He traveled with the wandering Israelites through the desert in a tent called the tabernacle; and the Word became flesh and dwelt among us one starry night in a Bethlehem stable. But the wonder of it all is that God never just showed up. He spoke to His people right in the midst of the busyness of their ordinary lives. He spoke to Moses while he was taking care of sheep; He spoke to the woman at the well while she was drawing water for her housework, and He spoke to Martha while she was busy preparing for her dinner guests.

All were ordinary people, each one hearing an extraordinary message on an otherwise uneventful day. Does that mean that God can speak to you? And to me? The question is not can He speak, but will we listen to His still, small voice. Henry Blackaby, in his book entitled *Experiencing God,* writes: "Right now God is working all around you and in your life. One of the greatest tragedies among God's people is that, while they have a deep longing to experience God, they are experiencing God day after day, but do not know how to recognize Him."

I haven't heard the Lord's voice from a burning bush lately. Nor have I been led through my journey by a pillar of fire. But God's presence is just as evident in my life. The stories that follow testify of that truth. They tell of sightings in the nooks and crannies of my home—in the kitchen as I've scrubbed the floor; in the family room, where I've caught a glimpse of what might have been but God said no, and even on the porch as I've opened the door to some unlikely guests.

Doesn't it make sense that we should find God in our homes where our hearts reside and seek sweet communion with our loved ones? John 1:14 says, "The Word became flesh, and dwelt among us." God moved into our hearts. He moved into our homes. Come now and walk with me through rooms filled with life, love, and laughter. Settle back and make yourself at home. I pray that you will catch glimpses of God's presence in your own life and feel . . . *At Home with God.*

—Sharon Jaynes

At Home with God

Stories of Life, Love, and Laughter

The Porch

Welcome to All

When I was a small child, I remember sitting in a sparsely decorated Sunday school room and musing over a solitary picture of Jesus that hung on the stark-white wall. In this picture, Jesus stood peacefully knocking at someone's door. I can remember wondering, *Why is He knocking? Isn't He God? Why doesn't He just walk on in?* I surmised that Jesus must have been a gentleman, who would never rush in where He wasn't welcome.

I also daydreamed about who lived on the other side of that door. Was it a family like my own, with a mommy, daddy, and two children? Or was it perhaps a grandma, who lived alone and waited anxiously for someone to stop by for a visit?

Other questions have occurred to me since: Is anyone home? What kind of house would Jesus visit? What would it be like to open your front door and find Jesus standing there?

If Jesus came to call at my house, He would first step up on my porch. I would hope He would pause a moment to enjoy the welcoming wreath and maybe even sit in the wicker rocking chair before ringing the bell. Above all, I'd want Him to feel welcome—at home and free to enter. But out of all my questions and musing, the most persistent thought was, *Who lives on the other side of that door where the Savior gently knocks?* Let's take a peek.

The Melting Pot

If you were going to knock on doors and invite guests to join you at the grandest wedding party of all time, whose doors would you choose? One day while visiting an amusement park with my son, I was reminded of just a few of the porches that Jesus might approach.

Going to an amusement park has never been amusing to me. Climbing a mountainous, rickety, wooden track, while clinging to the sides of a two-seater metal box with a flimsy bar across my lap for safety, and then plunging a hundred feet to the ground is not my idea of relaxation. And being herded through a roped maze and standing in line for hours to endure a ride that lasts ninety seconds is *definitely* not entertaining. Spinning in circles makes me nauseous.

Why then would I subject myself to such spinning, plunging, gyrating, and lunging into oblivion? The answer is simple; I love my family. I've endured roller coasters with my son, been turned upside down and spun in a corkscrew with my niece, and had my insides scrambled with my nephews—all to enjoy their smiles and make memories I'll never forget.

Amusement parks are the great melting pots of America. On one occasion while I was standing in a line waiting to become airborne on the death-defying "Gauntlet," I was struck by the sideshow of humanity surrounding me. A young teenage girl in minuscule cut-off shorts and a bikini bathing-suit top had covered her body in baby oil and glitter. We shared the same space with a potbellied motorcyclist, who had a skull and crossbones tattooed on his left shoulder, a ring through his pierced nose, and stringy blond hair hanging down his furry bare back. A group of snaggletoothed illiterates spit tobacco juice and watched it sizzle on the 101-degree asphalt.

While standing with my arms folded in disgust, queasy from the sights and smells of unwashed bodies and greasy hair, the Lord shed some light on my situation. He seemed to say, *Yes, you are clean and polished, standing here with manicured nails, pressed linen shorts, and a designer tee shirt. Your children reflect your lifestyle choices and upbringing. But I didn't come to the earth just for the lovely, neatly groomed, and freshly scented of society. I came for the foul-smelling shepherd, the leprous outcast, and the uneducated fisherman. I came for the glitter-covered girl, the nose-pierced gang member, and the snaggletoothed illiterate. These are all my sheep. I love each and every one of them just as much as I love you. They are all my children.*

My disgust turned to compassion. Jesus loved these people just as much as He loved me. He welcomed them and gave His life for them, just as He had for me.

I realized that instead of judging everyone by my standards, I should be using my time in line to pray. *Lord, whatever pain that young teen has experienced to cause her to dress so risquély and draw attention to herself, heal those hurts. Draw her to Yourself and help her to come to know You as her loving Father. May the man with the pierced nose one day have His heart pierced by the conviction of Your great love and sacrifice for him. May the snaggle-toothed illiterate be filled with the knowledge of Jesus Christ and Your will in all spiritual wisdom and understanding.*

My heart was filled with love for this merry band, and I was just about to call us together for a big group hug, when I realized it was time for my group to be loaded into our metal seat and strapped in place. Once again I was spun around at breakneck speed, turned on my head, and jerked to a sudden stop from sixty miles per hour. Fortunately, the thrill of my insights stayed with me throughout the ride, even if my lunch threatened not to.

Masterpiece by the Bay

Some of the porches where Jesus stands knocking belong to stately mansions with ornately carved gothic columns, raised panel oak doors, and polished brass hardware. And others belong to cinder-block structures with padded locks, rusty barbed wire, and iron bars that imprison hardened hearts. I stood on one such porch during a family trip to San Francisco.

I grew up on the East Coast and was excited when my family decided to visit this beautiful city for our vacation. One of the most amazing places we visited was the former maximum-security prison, Alcatraz. There in the middle of San Francisco Bay, just a mile and a quarter from the sights and sounds of this metropolitan city, sits a rock island, known by some as the Devil's Island of America or The Rock. From 1934 to 1963, Alcatraz housed the country's most corrupt, incorrigible criminals. Al Capone and Machine Gun Kelly were just two of its more infamous residents.

The only way to reach the prison is to ferry across the bay. As we taxied up to Alcatraz and stared at the shell of concrete walls, barbed wire, and iron bars, an eerie feeling crept over me. Each of us picked up a set of headphones and a cassette recorder and toured the prison while listening to the taped voices of various prisoners recounting their days behind bars. I walked into a cell called "the hole," closed my eyes, and tried to imagine what it would be like to live in solitary confinement with no light, no sound, and no other voice but my own. My heart was heavy as I thought about the souls that passed through those halls—souls full of darkness, depression, and despair.

But as I rounded the final corner of the tour, I saw a white-haired, eighty-year-old grandfather, with crystal-blue, laughing eyes, and a radiant smile that spread across his wrinkled face. A line formed as tourists stood waiting for him to sign his name and number on his autobiography, *Alcatraz: From the Inside.* This precious man was Jim Quillen, ex-prisoner #AZ586. He had spent ten years of his life, from 1942 to 1952, behind bars in this prison built to house the most dangerous criminals of his day. I looked in his eyes as we spoke.

This was not the face of a dangerous man. I wondered what had changed his life.

I didn't have to flip many pages in his book to find the answer. In it he wrote, "It was only through the grace of our Lord Jesus Christ and His intercession, that my life of hopeless incarceration was averted. His help and forgiveness permitted me to obtain freedom, family, and a useful and productive place in society." I sat down beside Mr. Quillen for a moment as God spoke to my heart, saying, *You prayed before coming here that you would see My handiwork and be reminded of My greatness. This man is some of my best work.*

On my trip to San Francisco, I was reminded of God's unchanging strength in the majestic rock cliffs of the shoreline and of His nurturing care as the Vinedresser in the hills of the Napa Valley wine country. I saw a picture of God's protective canopy over His children in the towering redwood forests. But when I looked into Jim Quillen's eyes, I saw God's most incredible masterpiece—a changed life. Because Jesus had knocked at the door of Mr. Quillen's heart, the ex-prisoner spent the rest of his life, welcoming and inviting others to meet the One who sets the prisoners free.

Potluck

I recall as a young child, rocking on my grandma's front porch and listening to the ladies from the missions' society gossip about the heathens whose church stood across the street from theirs. It always puzzled me, because the heathens were such nice people, and their church looked just like Grandma's. As far as I could tell, there was no difference. Both believed in Jesus, wore funny hats on Sundays, and sang the same hymns. And both had great potluck dinners.

How did the church come up with the notion of the infamous potluck supper (alias, covered-dish dinner)? As best as I can tell, it all began in the fifteenth chapter of Matthew. The first covered-dish gathering was a great success when Jesus served more than four thousand men (not to mention a few thousand women and children) and had leftovers to boot. All this came from one little covered dish. Actually, it was a covered basket. This was, after all, before the advent of Corningware.

Later the Baptists followed His lead, and the next thing you know, all the denominations were celebrating a multiplicity of occasions with every variety of casserole known to man. But the twenty-first century church wouldn't be caught just serving up fish and chips. No, we have taken the notion of breaking bread and run with it. Not only do we break bread, but we crunch fried chicken, munch fresh veggies, scoop casseroles, slice pies, cut cakes, and sip coffees. We chew the fat while chewing our food and extend the right hand of fellowship while our left hand extends the serving spoon. No matter how much food walks through the doors, none ever goes to waste, but much goes to the *waist.* Covered-dish dinners are one of the most cherished rituals in the church today.

One Christmas our Sunday school held a potluck dinner party at the home of Dr. and Mrs. Marshall McMillian. Our class consisted of a hundred and fifty people in a church of sixteen hundred. Since it's a little difficult to be intimate with a hundred and fifty congregates on Sunday morning, the Christmas party was a great time to chat with people you didn't normally have

a chance to meet. Because people tend to sit in the same seats every week, I'd never actually gotten a good look at about half of the class. The Christmas party was designed to remedy that problem.

The McMillians beautifully decorated their home with holly, spruce, and magnolia clippings. It was filled with the sights, sounds, and smells of the season, which included the incoming aroma of the many deliciously prepared meals. In an effort to provide crowd control and proper traffic flow, our host, Marshall, posted directional signs around the house. One sign read COATS, with an arrow pointing up the stairs to their daughter's room. Another read HOT FOOD, with an arrow pointing toward the kitchen.

Marshall stood at the door, carrying out his job as official greeter and traffic cop.

"Hello, how are you?" He smiled and greeted two ladies and a man as they made their way up the front steps with dishes in hand. "You can take your food into the kitchen and then follow the arrows up the stairs to the coat room."

The obedient threesome followed directions well and then headed to the nametag table. But a warning light flashed through my mind.

"Marshall," I said, "Who are those people? I don't recognize them."

"I don't recognize them, either," he answered. "But you know how big our class is. Maybe they sit on the opposite side of the room, and we just haven't noticed them before."

They looked like they could have been one of us. They seemed to know the drill. But something was wrong with this picture.

"Marshall, go find out who they are," I urged.

He approached the trio, all of whom were now looking a little bewildered. "Excuse me, you *are* here for the Sunday school Christmas party, aren't you?"

"Yes," they answered. However, their "yes" sounded more like a question than an answer. Then they asked, "This is the Sunday school class for First Baptist Church, isn't it?"

"No, ma'am," Marshall answered. "This is the party for Forest Hill Presbyterian. You folks are at the wrong party."

Quickly, the three embarrassed Baptists reclaimed their food, once again followed the arrows to the coat room, and hightailed it out of the McMillians' house to another Sunday school covered-dish gathering a few doors down.

Won't heaven be an interesting place? It will be one big, perpetual, brightly-lit Christmas party—a celebration of new birth. No covered dish will be required because God will seat us at the banqueting table that He has already prepared for us. And the great thing about this party will be that when the Baptists stumble into a roomful of Presbyterians, no one will feel out of place. We will all say, "Welcome! Come on in. Take off your coat and stay a while—an eternity for that matter. You're definitely in the right place."

It's What's on the Inside that Counts

The doorbell rang, and I sprang to my feet to answer it. The courier was already driving away before I had a chance to thank him for the return of a missing suitcase, one that had gone astray during a visit to Mexico. I looked at the delivery he had left on my front porch and thanked God for His latest reminder of how much He values those who open the doors of their hearts to Him.

My husband, son, and I traveled to Cancun, Mexico during spring break in 1996. The vacation was a fun family time, but the trip home was grueling. The airport was full of hot, sweaty, smelly vacationers anxious to return home. We were originally scheduled to leave

Mexico at 5:30 P.M., but because of various delays, the flight was rescheduled for 8:30 P.M. When the plane finally arrived, the darkness of the night could not hide the fact that the aircraft was old, dirty, and decrepit. Yet the hot plane was filled to capacity. It didn't matter that the flight crew spoke little English, because the plane was so loud that we couldn't hear what was said anyway. We couldn't even hear the person in the seat beside us. My son kept insisting, "Mom, when we walked by the plane to get on, I saw duct tape on the left rear wing!"

We knew we were in trouble when we put down our tray tables and two of the three were broken. When the flight attendant demonstrated the emergency procedures, we all paid *very* close attention. As a matter of fact, I don't think I ever remember seeing such an attentive group of passengers. My son and I even practiced.

After we were finally airborne, the flight attendant announced that because of flight delays, the Charlotte customs office, our final destination, would be closed when we arrived. So we had to stop over in Florida at the Orlando airport to go through U.S. customs.

At midnight, ninety hot, tired, disgruntled passengers disembarked, checked their carry-ons through customs, picked up their luggage at the baggage claim, checked that luggage through customs, then returned to board the same rickety plane.

This didn't sound too complicated, especially since we were the only people in the whole Orlando airport at midnight! There was just one problem. One of our suitcases, containing my husband and son's dirty clothes, did not make it to baggage claim. It was missing, probably somewhere back in Mexico. We were a little upset, but at that point, we were more concerned with getting home in one piece. Finally, we landed in Charlotte at 2:15 A.M. and filled out the necessary claim form for lost luggage, hoping for the best. We were not terribly perturbed. After all, it was only clothes, and dirty ones at that.

The next day as he settled down for some quiet time, my husband reached for his Bible. But it was nowhere to be found.

"Honey, have you seen my Bible?" he asked. "I can't find it anywhere!" As soon as he finished his sentence, he remembered where he had put it. His Bible was in the lost suitcase with all the dirty clothes. Suddenly, the suitcase was no longer unimportant. This was the Bible that I had given to him on our honeymoon fifteen years earlier, the Bible that I had rebound on our tenth anniversary, the Bible with study notes written on every page. We began to pray. We called and asked others to pray. We *had* to get that suitcase back!

As I spoke to the Lord about the suitcase, He spoke to my heart, *Isn't it amazing how the realization of what was inside the suitcase changed its value? So it is with My people. You may look at someone and see only filthy rags, but I see a beautiful creation and a possible dwelling place for My Son, and that makes them valuable.*

Never again will I look at the dirty and downtrodden the same way. I realized that day that each person has great value as a possible container of something—Someone—very special, Jesus Christ, God's own Son. He stands at the doors of many who, in our eyes, may appear as lost luggage, filled with filthy rags. But now when I see such a person, I try to imagine, as though I had X-ray vision, a little black Bible hidden somewhere among the clutter, and I can see them as my Heavenly Father sees them—welcomed, valuable, and precious in His sight.

* *The airport courier delivered our suitcase four days later—Bible intact!*

Just Say No to Neighbors

I hate to admit it, but there have been times when I have pulled in my welcome mat from the front porch. Once a neighbor became furious with me for correcting her child. She called and told me what a terrible person I was. Who did I think I was for correcting her little angel? I won't go into all the gory details, but let's just say she was less than flattering. I did apologize but decided on a new no-nonsense policy for dealing with my neighbors.

"Lord, I have a plan," I said. "Here's the deal. I am *not* going to make friends with any of my neighbors. I am going to keep to myself, stay in my own yard, and play with my own toys. I'm going to remove the welcome mat at the front door and make sure the alarm-system warning sticker is displayed in a prominent place. No borrowing a cup of sugar. No talking over the fence. No *anything!* I am even going to import Steven's playmates. This 'Just Say No to Neighbors' policy is in effect immediately."

The next day, I dropped my son off at a YMCA basketball camp. At pick-up time, we moms were standing around talking while waiting for our sons. There was a pretty blonde there, and I heard someone ask where she lived. "I've just moved from the Myers Park area of town to Stratfordshire Drive in the Matthews area," she said. Then she looked over at me and smiled.

That was my street! She *knew* I had heard her, and she *knew* I lived on that street. I politely returned her smile and felt panic creep in. What was I supposed to do? My new policy had been in effect for less than forty-eight hours!

I told God that I would introduce myself, but I reminded Him of my "Just Say No to Neighbors" policy. After all, I did not want to be rude, just distant . . . okay, safe. I introduced myself to Debi, welcomed her to the neighborhood, and chatted for a few minutes. Then I grabbed my son by the shirt and scurried away.

That afternoon there was a knock at the door. When I looked out the window, guess who was standing on my porch? None other than my new cheerful neighbor, Debi, just dropping by to say hello. As I opened the door, I again reminded the Lord of my plan, just in case He had forgotten. My guard stayed up for about five minutes after she strolled into my house.

Debi walked into the sunroom and exclaimed, "Oh look, we have the same china pattern. And I see you like to collect things with bunnies on them. I just love bunnies, don't you? I have them all over my house. Oh look, we even have some of the *same* bunnies!"

We discovered that we both enjoyed decorative flags and had one for each month of the year. Then with a luminous smile, Debi said, "You know, when we moved in and I saw the cute flag with firecrackers hanging by your porch, I just knew we would be friends." And we have been ever since that day. We go to flea markets together and reach for the same items. We paint together, look for bargains together, and go on garden tours together. And although I had been quite capable before, I could no longer make any home decorating decision without first getting her opinion.

My "Just Say No to Neighbors" plan lasted less than two days. Since then, I have opened my heart and home to other neighbors, and many have become my extended family. I'm so glad that God ignores my silly resolves. After all, it's His house too.

Someone's Knocking

Once there was a little girl who lived in an upper-middle class neighborhood in eastern North Carolina. Thirty-foot pine trees shaded the long, ranch-style porch with rounded columns, brick-paved floor, and a welcoming red door. The azaleas and immaculate lawn portrayed a picture of tranquillity, but inside the walls of her home, the atmosphere brewed with hostility and fear.

Her father was a successful businessman who spent little time with the family. When he was home, he drank heavily, and her parents fought both verbally and physically in her presence. Many nights, she would lie in bed with the covers pulled tightly under her chin, praying that she would quickly fall asleep to shut out the sound of her parents' yelling. Her parents did indeed love the child, but because they were so miserable with themselves and their marriage, they had a hard time knowing how to express that love.

When she was twelve years old, the little girl, who was no longer so little, began spending a lot of time with her best friend, Wanda Henderson. Wanda's mother took the child under her wing and loved her like she was her own daughter. Mrs. Henderson knew about the home with its broken lives and occasional broken furniture. And she knew about the girl's broken heart.

Mr. and Mrs. Henderson had a great marriage. They hugged and kissed each other in front of the children, and even called each other by pet names. For the first time in her life, the little girl saw what a relationship between husband and wife was supposed to be like. She didn't understand all the reasons that their home was so full of love and so strikingly different from her own, but she knew that the difference had something to do with God.

One day, Mrs. Henderson asked if the girl would like to attend church with her family. A really cute boy sang in the youth choir, so she eagerly agreed. The next year, Mrs. Henderson started a Bible study for teens, and the girl never missed a meeting, devouring every word like a hungry student. Then one night, when the girl was fourteen, Mrs. Henderson asked her if she was ready to accept Jesus Christ as her personal Savior. The young girl remembered a picture of Jesus that she had seen hanging on the stark white wall of her Sunday school class some ten years earlier—a picture of Him standing at a door, knocking, and waiting to come in. She realized at that moment, the door was indeed the door of her heart.

So that night, the young girl opened the door and welcomed Jesus into her heart, and He forever changed her life. In case you haven't guessed, that little girl was me. Three years later, my mother gave her life to Christ, and two years after that, my father also committed his life to the Lord. I've never gotten over the wonder of what can happen when you open a door. A whole new world could be waiting.

Jesus still knocks on doors. Perhaps He's knocking on yours. Maybe you invited Him in years ago, but as the house got mussed, you ran out of time to pay attention to Him. Or you wanted to pursue other activities and you pushed Him out the door. Now as He knocks, what will you say? Why not welcome Him to cross the threshold of your heart and invite Him to take up residence in your home?

Dear Lord,

Thank You for still knocking on doors today, desiring not just to stop by for a visit on the porch, but to abide with us and in us. May I welcome You in every day and into every room of my dwelling and my heart! Thank You for giving me a glimpse of who lives behind all the closed doors and showing me more of what You meant when you said, "For God so loved the world, that He gave His only begotten Son" (John 3:16).

Give me a welcoming spirit, one that will open the door of my heart to share Your love with all Your precious sheep who wander my way: the lost sheep, the prize sheep, and even the black sheep.

Amen.

Elise
2000

The Kitchen

Sustenance for Life

The bouquet of cinnamon potpourri simmers on the stove, the aroma of newly ground espresso beans wafts from the coffeemaker, and the yeasty scent of baking bread rises from the oven. As the morning sun cavorts into my kitchen, the bird songs are floating through an open window in a cool breeze. Whether it's muffins at daybreak, peanut butter and jelly at noon, scones at teatime, or roast at day's end, this is the place where bodies are refueled and souls are recharged.

And it is the Word of God that nourishes our spirits to face each new day with confidence, assurance, and expectancy. It is the Bread of Life that gives us sustenance for living. Come sit at my table to "taste and see that the LORD is good" (Psalm 34:8).

How's Your Reception?

"Steve! Steven! Dinner's ready."

Have you ever worked diligently to prepare a scrumptious dinner and had everything timed just perfectly, the rolls lightly browned just as the buzzer for the soufflé signals it's time to come out of the oven, the roast at the perfect temperature, and the congealed salad standing at attention? Then you call your brood: "Steve! Steven! Dinner's ready!" No response.

A few minutes elapse. "Steve! Steven! Dinner's ready!" More time passes, and there's still no response.

This has happened many times at the Jaynes' household. As my temper rises and the warm dinner cools, I've often thought about how frustrated God must feel when He calls out to us and gets no response. The Lord taught me a little lesson in how to be a better listener through a gift from my son.

When Steven was thirteen years old, he was appalled at my lack of technological advancement in the area of communication. In other words, he thought I was still living in the Dark Ages because I didn't have a car phone. But I didn't want a car phone. My station wagon was one place where I could get away from the telephone's constant pull on my attention, so I settled for just not being "with it." Besides, he really just wanted me to have one so he could call into the local radio station and win prizes on our drive to school each morning.

"Mom, why don't you have a car phone? Everybody else has one."

"Everyone?" I asked. "Your dad doesn't have one."

"Okay, Dad doesn't. But tell me another mom, besides Grandma, who doesn't," he argued.

Actually, his grandmother *did* have one, but I did not feel this was the time to share that information with him. "I just don't need a car phone, Son, and being able to call the radio station to win prizes is not a good reason to pay monthly service fees. End of subject."

Boy, was I surprised that Christmas when I opened my lovely present from Steven to discover a flip-top cell phone purchased with his own money. How could I not appear grateful for a gift from my own child (that sly dog)? Of course the activation fee and monthly billing were not included in the deal. He had convinced my husband that it wasn't safe for me to drive all around town without a phone. So Steve agreed to pay the monthly fees. This gift reminded me of the man who gives his wife a power saw for her birthday. I definitely needed to give him a few lessons on how to shop for a woman.

"Thank you, Steven," I said. "Now whenever Dad and I are out and you are home alone, I can call you anytime, from anyplace, to see what you're doing." From the look on his face, I could tell that the thought had never crossed his mind.

A few weeks later, I decided to try out my new toy.

"Steven, this is Mom. Dad and I are in the car. When I hang up, I want you to call this number and let's see if the phone works."

"Okay," he said as we hung up.

We waited about three minutes, but the phone never rang.

"Steven, this is Mom again. What happened?"

"I called the number," he explained, "but the operator said that your phone was turned off or that you were out of the calling area."

"That can't be right. I'm ten miles from home, and the phone is definitely ON. Try again."

Steven tried again, but the results were the same. The call would not go through. The next day, I called the telephone company and explained what had happened the night before.

"Mrs. Jaynes, where were you when you tried to receive the call?"

"I was on Randolph Road, near Central Church," I answered.

"Let me explain something," she ventured. "A cellular phone works by sending out and receiving radio waves from a cell tower. You were at a point on Randolph Road that dips and forms a small valley, and the radio waves could not reach down into the dip for you to receive the signal.

"Another possibility is that your message was being blocked by a large building, maybe even the church. We have problems uptown where large buildings block signals all the time. And finally, Mrs. Jaynes, was your battery powered up? Had you charged it lately?"

"Yes," I answered. "I had charged it that very day."

"And the antenna was up?"

"Yes," I said, a little more than perturbed at all the parameters and requirements. "The antenna was up."

"Let me get this straight," I summarized. "I am now the owner of a flip-top cellular phone for the purpose of reaching my son any time, any place. However, for it to work properly, I must not be behind tall buildings or in a dip in the road. Also, I must keep it fully charged and outside of my purse with the antenna up."

"That's pretty much it," she answered.

"But why is it," I added, "that I can always send a call, but I am having trouble receiving a call?"

"Well, Mrs. Jaynes, it takes more signal strength to receive a call than to send a call."

I was more than frustrated with this two-by-six-inch piece of plastic and power cells, but it made me consider other transmissions that I had trouble receiving from time to time. The Scripture says in John 10:27 that the Lord speaks to His sheep and His sheep hear His voice. But why do I have so much trouble hearing from God? Could it be the same reasons that I have poor reception with my cellular phone?

If I'm having trouble hearing from God, I have to ask myself the same questions that the cell phone operator asked me. Am I perhaps in a dip in the road? Sometimes a valley of depression or a case of the blues can clog my spiritual ears in such a way that I don't hear His gentle voice coaxing me to higher ground. If that is the case, I need to start singing praises like David did in the Psalms and watch Him turn my valley into a level path.

Have I erected walls that are blocking God's signals: walls of materialism, selfish ambition, or religion? If so, I need to tear them down. Is my battery pack powered up? If not, I need to plug into his Word and get recharged. Is my antenna raised or have I put it down like the Israelites who, because of fear, told Moses, "Speak to us yourself and we will listen. But do not have God speak to us" (Exodus 20:19 NIV). If I want to hear from Him, I need to make sure that my spiritual antenna is up and that I am expectantly waiting to hear His voice.

Finally, why is it that I can always place a call but I sometimes have trouble receiving a call? I can go before the Lord at any time and He hears my cry. It doesn't take more *power* to receive a message from Him, but it does take more *effort* on my part to be receptive. In

Psalm 46:10 NIV, it says, "Be still, and know that I am God." In this fast-paced world in which we live, it takes much more effort to stand still and listen than it does to speak. But I need to realize that what the Lord has to say to me is much more important than anything I have to say to Him. Perhaps that's why He gave us two ears but only one mouth!

I held my little flip-top phone in the palm of my hand and thanked God for visiting and showing me once again how to hear His voice. Steven's gift had turned out to be of much greater value than even he could have imagined. What I realized was that hearing from the Lord was more than just receiving; it was also about making myself receptive. And that is the basis for obtaining true sustenance for life. Dinner's ready! Will you come?

Confidence to Bank On

Many women have admitted to me that though they have a sincere desire to open up their homes for dinner guests, they are reluctant because they feel inadequate as cooks. That lack of confidence in the kitchen has kept many from sharing meals to nourish the body, but more importantly, it has kept many from sharing the sustenance found in Christ that nourishes the soul.

As a teen, I was never a particularly confident person, but I did learn how to act like I was when I went to dental hygiene school. The instructors taught us, "Now girls, when the patients come into the clinic for their cleaning appointments, you must act confident. You must act like you know what you are doing, even if you don't. If you act nervous, it will make the patients nervous."

For the first semester, I didn't have to worry about appearing confident because our only client was a mannequin named Dexter. But then came the "real people"—real patients. I found that real people were different from my friend Dexter. They did not have levers on the tops of their heads to pull when I wanted them to open, and I could not fold up their tongue or pin it to their cheeks when it got in the way. And it was part of my job to make these real people feel comfortable.

I made it through dental hygiene school, and the art of acting self-assured, even when I wasn't, proved useful on several occasions in my adult life. My husband, Steve, and I got married while we were still in college and had few funds for a honeymoon. With yard-sale money, we took a quick trip to the Outer Banks of North Carolina, just three hours from my hometown. On our seventh anniversary, we decided to finally take that honeymoon trip, a cruise in the Bahamas. It was my job to make most of the travel preparations, which included purchasing traveler's checks from the bank. I had never used traveler's checks and didn't really know what to do. I didn't even know what a traveler's check looked like.

At this point, my "act confident even if you don't know what you are doing" training kicked in. I walked into the bank, and confidently, like I had done this a million times, announced to the teller, "I would like to buy some traveler's checks."

Without looking up, she asked, "What denomination?"

I thought that was a strange question, but answered, "Presbyterian. We go to a Presbyterian church."

The teller looked up, the corners of her lips curled into a sardonic grin, as she said, "No, honey. I mean, do you want your checks in tens, twenties, or fifties."

My confidence level plummeted and hovered somewhere below zero. I felt myself shrinking before the teller's eyes as she enlightened me on a new word for the day. As I tried to find my voice, I squeaked, "Twenties will be fine." As she prepared the traveler's checks, I tried to remember the Bible verses about the moneychangers. I did not like this woman.

After I received my traveler's checks, in denominations of twenty, I scurried out of the bank, never to return. I'm sure she still tells that story at office parties and family reunions and will probably tell it to her grandchildren. My confidence was shattered. This time, my strategy had not worked.

In the car, I leaned my head on the steering wheel. I had never felt so mortified. Then the Lord reminded me of where my true confidence lies. "Put no confidence in the flesh," Paul said in Philippians 3:3. And, "I am confident of this very thing, that He who began a good work in you will perfect it until the day of Christ Jesus (Philippians 1:6)." Now that's real confidence, and you can take that to the bank!

Led Astray

When I think back to all the rooms in my home that have been a refuge to so many, it's my kitchen that stands out above the rest. Whether it's sharing a hot cup of coffee with a wife whose marriage has grown cold, a warm bowl of soup with a teen whose emotions are going haywire, or a cold glass of iced tea with a husband whose temper needs to cool, my kitchen table has been the springboard for listening, consolation, and prayer. A great number of the hurts I've listened to have been the result of someone choosing to go astray. And just how easily that can happen was illustrated in the fate of one of my dog's puppies.

One spring, we decided to let our golden retriever, Ginger, get "married." Shortly thereafter, she gave birth to seven golden balls of fur—two males and five females. I called one of the adoptive parents just a few hours after delivery.

"Cynthia, this is Sharon. The puppies are here! We have the pick of the litter set aside for you—a fine fat butterball of a male. What shall we call him?"

"Fletcher!" her three children yelled in the background.

Seven weeks and many bags of Puppy Chow later, we delivered Fletcher to the Shangri-La of the dog world. Our friends, Larry and Cynthia Price, and their three children, live in a home surrounded by thirty acres of undeveloped forest land. As we drove down their mile-long driveway carved through the sixty-foot pines, I imagined Fletcher thinking of his siblings and musing, *If they could only see me now!*

For the next seven years, Fletcher's days consisted of roaming through the forest, sniffing out snakes and raccoons, chasing deer and terrifying their young, and taking naps with possums or any other creature that happened to wander into the Price's backyard. On days that he got overheated from all his adventures, he practiced his dog paddling in the nearby pond. His only concern in life was Larry and the tweezers that he used nightly to remove ticks that hitchhiked on their furry host.

One day, Cynthia got a call from a friend in the city. "Cynthia, this is Lynette. We're going out of town for a week, and I hate to put our dog in the kennel for that long. Would you mind if she came out to your place and spent the week while we're gone?"

"Sure, bring her on over. Fletcher will like the company." And boy, did he!

Adam had Eve. Samson had Delilah. Now Fletcher had Roxy.

After being properly introduced and sniffing each other in a circular motion for fifteen minutes, the two new friends were off and running. Fletcher commenced to show Roxy the ropes of country living. *Here's how you chase a deer. Watch out for those hooves! These snakes are really cool to bark at. How about this pond mud! I bet you don't have anything like this in the city.* The dogs were a furry blur of activity.

Two days later, Cynthia noticed the couple bounding down the mile-long driveway, only this time, Roxy was in the lead. A few hours later, the family realized that the two dogs were gone. For the first time in seven years, Fletcher had left the safety and security of his haven, led astray by his new friend.

Larry and the kids searched everywhere, but came up empty-handed. After a sleepless night, Cynthia had an idea. Even though the Boyds, Roxy's owners, had moved from their house in town nearly three years ago, she had a hunch to drive by their old address.

"Fletcher! Roxy!" she called from her car window in front of her neighbor's former address.

Slowly but surely, two filthy mutts emerged from under the house with tails tucked and heads hanging low.

"You bad dogs," Cynthia chided. "Get in the car this instant!"

Cynthia drove the two renegades home and promptly chained Roxy to a tree. "Girl, your vacation is definitely over."

The next day, Larry went outside to feed Fletcher and his wayward friend, but Fletcher was gone. Again, they searched the streets, the highways, and even their friend's old street. But this time, there was no dog. This time, their pet was gone for good.

Before Roxy, Fletcher had lived a happy and contented life, without a care in the world. His abode was the dog version of the Garden of Eden, surrounded by a loving family and with every possible desire right at his paw tips. But then a new buddy came along and wanted to show him that there was more to life than the secure confines of the thirty-acre woods. The enticing Roxy led her stable companion astray. Once he had tasted the forbidden fruit, once he had sniffed the foreign smells, the pull toward the tempting new land was too strong.

What a picture of temptation! 1 Corinthians 15:33 NIV says, "Do not be misled: 'Bad company corrupts good character.'" And the Amplified version states it this way, "Do not be so deceived and misled! Evil companionships, (communion, associations) corrupt *and* deprave good manners *and* morals *and* character." When we allow someone to lead us into an area where we should not go, to eat a fruit that we should not eat, to gaze upon that which we should not look, or to seek sustenance from some source besides God, we are setting ourselves up as strays instead of members of a loving family. The temptation may appear exciting and adventurous at first, but the end is scavenging for what was once freely given—love, nourishment, protection, and a sense of belonging—all the things that sustain our souls.

The Perm

We all know the table etiquette rule, "Don't talk with your mouth full." But I've decided we need a prayer etiquette rule that says, "Don't pray with your mind full." We need to get away from the noise of life and concentrate on hearing His still small voice.

One of the loudest places that I know of is the hair salon. My hair is stick straight with zero body. It was the perfect hair for the sixties, when straight hair parted down the middle like the Red Sea was in style. But now that I'm all grown up, I take all kinds of drastic measures to make sure that my hair does *not* lay flat on my head. One of my biannual rituals is getting a perm. There are three ways that you can tell that I've just had a permanent: French poodles tend to stop and stare, wondering if I am one of their long-lost relatives; my

family walks about ten paces behind me with clothespins on their noses, and I have a red stripe across my forehead near my hairline.

For some reason, the skin on my forehead is sensitive, and the perm solution has a tendency to burn a red stripe just below my hairline. The last time I went in for this session in vanity, Barbara, my hairdresser, put petroleum jelly across this area to avoid the "mark of the beast." After winding my hair on a thousand tiny rods, she applied a neutralizing solution and placed me under a hair dryer to process. In the meantime, I processed what was going on around me in the beauty salon. It was wall-to-wall with women, some with their heads in sinks and some reading with their heads under hair dryers.

I was sitting there thinking about how ridiculous we all looked when Barbara walked up and asked, "How's your corn bread?"

How's my corn bread? What a crazy question! I leaned out from under the roar of the dryer and asked, "What did you say?"

She repeated, "How's your forehead?"

I told her that I thought she had said, "How's your corn bread?" Everyone started laughing. But the amazing thing is that for the next thirty minutes, everyone talked about corn bread. Some liked the middle square. Some liked the corners. Some liked it with buttermilk. Some liked it crumbled up in milk. It went on and on. A whole treatise developed on the joys of corn bread.

Still observing and processing, I thought of how many times a life is changed by something someone *thought* someone else said. Walls have been built and friendships destroyed over misunderstandings. And even when the error is corrected, some keep discussing, mulling over, and ruminating on what they *thought* they heard.

As the dryer roared in my ears, I thought about how God must feel when He speaks to His sheep and our heads are in such a noisy place that we can't tell exactly what He's saying. A Martha, busy in the kitchen, might hear, "How's your corn bread?" But a listening Mary might correctly hear, "How's your forehead?" I need to make sure that when I'm listening to the Lord, I get my head out from under the noise and hear Him correctly.

I may have left that day with a perm in my hair and a red mark across the top of my forehead. But I also left with a renewed desire to listen closely to the Father's voice, so He can leave a permanent mark on my heart.

Emergency! Emergency!

I love to prepare nutritious meals for my family. But I detest feeling like a short-order cook, whose sole purpose in life is to slave away in the kitchen, supplying food on demand. Yet, sometimes I selfishly expect God to cater to my needs in the same way.

My husband, Steve, graduated from dental school in 1981. I was his only employee: his dental hygienist, dental assistant, receptionist, and insurance clerk. On the days that I was not helping him, I worked for another dentist in town. I was so exhausted most of the time that our joke became, "Sharon works six days a week and cries on the seventh."

One thing that amazed me in starting a new practice was all of the emergency phone calls that Steve received on nights and weekends. Once the phone rang at about two o'clock in the morning. I groggily picked up the receiver and managed a weak, "Hello."

"Hello," the woman on the other end stated. "My son is having a terrible toothache. Is the doctor in?"

Where else did she think he would be at two o'clock in the morning? "Yes ma'am, he is. How long has this tooth been bothering your son?"

"Oh, I'd say for about two weeks," she answered.

So why did you wait until NOW to call, I thought! Then I asked, "Ma'am, how old is your son?"

She answered, "Twenty-seven. My son is twenty-seven years old."

I was so shocked that I quickly sat up in bed, accidentally jerking the phone cord out of the wall and disconnecting the caller. She did not call back. I had envisioned a distraught mother with a crying five-year-old child. But twenty-seven?

I lay back down, complaining and grumbling, "God, why is it that people won't go to the doctor regularly and only want help on demand when they have an emergency?"

When I got quiet enough to listen, the Lord spoke to my heart, "Now you know how I feel."

Let's Joust, Daddy!

Fast food from a drive through, eaten while driving on the freeway: Doesn't that just conjure up warm, fuzzy feelings of . . . indigestion and heartburn? Yet it's most Americans idea of dinner these days. However, studies have shown that families who eat at least one meal together per day produce children who are more academically successful and less likely to break the law. Similarly in God's family, His children who share at least one meal with Him per day are more victorious spiritually and less likely to break His law. But sometimes finding the time to sit down together as a family demands sacrifice.

In 1986, my husband and I built a house that was to be our last stop before the retirement home or the loony bin, whichever came first. While the builders were hammering away, I was sewing away, trying to have all the curtains made before we moved in.

The fabric for the curtains came on five-foot-long cardboard tubes. For a solid year, those tubes were my two-year-old son's favorite toys. They served as tunnels for tiny cars and giant megaphones from which all sorts of important announcements were made. But jousting (swordplay) was his favorite thing to do with the tubes. Everyday when my husband, Steve, came home from work, he was greeted by little Steven shouting, "Let's joust, Daddy!" My husband jousted tirelessly for months.

Nine years later, in a conversation remembering the jousting days, my son confessed, "You know, I used to have terrible nightmares about those huge cardboard tubes. When I was two, I used to dream that giant jousting rods were chasing me all around the house trying to get me."

Baffled, I asked him, "Why didn't you tell us about the dreams then? And why did you want to continue to play with the tubes if they gave you bad dreams?"

"I guess it was because I loved Dad so much and playing the game with him," he answered, "that it was worth having the scary dreams."

Little did Steven know what a profound statement he had just made! My thoughts immediately went to my Heavenly Father, my love for Him, and what I was willing to endure to spend time with Him. I have a jousting rod, too. It is called the "sword of the spirit, which is the word of God" (Ephesians 6:17). I love to joust with my Heavenly Daddy. This jousting does not cause me to have bad dreams, but sometimes I have to endure a house that's not as clean as I would like or a project that is in the other room, screaming out to be finished. That's a nightmare to me.

In this busy world in which we live, taking time out to be with our Father, to feed on His Word and be nourished in His presence, can be somewhat of a struggle. But the rewards are so great. So every morning, I grab my jousting rod, God's Word, and say, "Let's joust, Daddy." The only difference is that my Father and I are not fighting against each other, but side by side, and His Word gives me the sustenance I need to meet the challenges of each new day.

No Clams for Larry

Sometimes we like what life serves to us, and sometimes we don't. But most of the time, it simply depends on the attitude of the person holding the spoon. Such was the case one evening when I went out to dinner with friends to the Sanitary Fish Market. I know that is a strange name for a seafood restaurant, but it was a great place that everyone frequented in Atlantic Beach, North Carolina. Since the food was good, I guess it was an added perk to know it was sanitary as well.

When I was eighteen, one evening I went out to dinner with three friends. Three of us were Christians, but the fourth thought we were ridiculous for believing in the whole religious thing. Larry preferred the macho, "I'm in control of my destiny" approach to life. But we loved him anyway.

The three of us usually took a moment to ask a blessing before we ate a meal, but we had never before eaten in a restaurant with Larry. He thought that surely, we would not pray in a public place and embarrass him completely. Well, we did. But not Larry. He held his head high as if to say, "I might be at the same table with these people, but I'm not one of them."

All four of us ordered clam chowder as an appetizer. We had the same waitress and the same chowder from the same pot. We three "holy rollers," as Larry called us, dipped our spoons into our bowls and tasted chowder full of tender clams and steamy potatoes.

Then proud Larry dipped in his spoon and retrieved only broth. "Why is your chowder full of clams and stuff," he demanded, "and all I've got is juice?"

Larry was about to exercise his macho mania and call the waitress over to complain when I looked up and said, "Well, maybe it's because we blessed ours and you didn't."

Larry didn't complain to the fine people at the Sanitary, but ate "crow" instead. Maybe sometimes when our "life soup" seems watery and without substance, before we complain to the management, we need to make sure we've talked to the Boss!

** The names in this story have been changed to protect the innocent . . . and not so innocent.*

A Watched Pot Never Burns

You've heard the expression that "a watched pot never boils." Well I must say, I've taken that maxim to heart, and as a result, ruined several good cooking utensils and burned many pots of water. How do you "burn water" you ask? It's simple. First you put water in a pot and turn the temperature to high. Since the water will not boil if you watch it, you leave the room to answer the telephone, fold a load of laundry, or run out to get the mail. One thing leads to another, and thirty minutes later, you remember the boiling water. When you return, you discover an empty, warped, blackened saucepan. This result is most wonderfully observed when heating a copper-bottom pot for at least one hour. Black flakes fall from the charred copper and float to the floor as you remove the abandoned pot from the stove's heat. Once you burn a pot, everything you cook in it after that comes out a little on the gray side.

Every time I've ruined a pot and had to throw it away, I've vowed to watch over my brew more carefully. But inevitably, the phone rings or someone comes to the door, and *voila*—another pot fatality.

After six of these catastrophes, the discarded pots were eating into my household budget. I had a few options, one of which was to buy a whistling teakettle. *What a pleasant little song my kettle will sing as it notifies me it's time for tea!* I thought. It was so cute with its shiny, new metal, curved, slender handle and round copper bottom. But the song it sang was anything but sweet. When the steam built up, that kettle let out an angry shrill that made my dog howl and my family yell at me to "get that thing off of there!" When my little teakettle got all steamed up and I heard her high-pitched whistle, I had to sprint from wherever I was in the house to rescue my family's ears. But at least I had stopped burning pots.

After a few months of ear-piercing reminders and mad dashes to the kitchen, I made a new discovery. I found out that if I pushed the button that made the teakettle's spout open, just halfway down and a smidgen to the right, it would catch on the lip of the spout and stay open just far enough to let the steam out so that it wouldn't whistle.

You can guess what happened. About two weeks later, I left the room and returned to a charred, empty pot rocking back and forth on the stove's hot eye. After it cooled off, it went to pot heaven—the local landfill.

With burnt-pot number seven, I finally learned my lesson. Of course, we all know that a watched pot will indeed boil—sooner or later. However, it tests our patience. Watching seems like such a terrible waste of time to me, but that's not what the Scripture says. Shepherds watched over their flocks by night; guardsmen watched over their people by patrolling the city walls, and the Proverbs 31 woman watched over the affairs of her household and her lamp did not go out at night.

The woman who watches over the affairs of her household, guards, protects, saves, and attends to the people most precious to her. That is certainly not a waste of time. In addition to watching over our family's physical needs, more importantly, we are watching over their emotional and spiritual needs. We are providing the sustenance of God's Word for their spirits, along with the sustenance of food for their growing bodies. We are bathing them in prayer, listening to their successes and failures, and paying attention to their outside interests and friends. We may never know how many disasters have been averted by our prayers, availability, and nurturing care. But if we become distracted by all the other activities that scream for our attention, the pot may burn.

I've put a new maxim in place in my home: A watched pot will, indeed, boil—but a watched pot will never burn.

Thank You, Lord, for My Dirty Floor

Do you sometimes get tired of the endless hours of housework? The washing . . . the ironing . . . the dusting . . . the cooking . . . the washing again?

One day while mopping the kitchen floor, I was in a cranky mood. Then I had a thought. Suppose I was blind and couldn't see the beautiful patterns on the linoleum floor, or the spilled juice by the refrigerator, or the crumbs under the baby's chair? If I were deaf, I couldn't hear the soothing sound of the soap bubbles, dissolving in my scrub bucket. I couldn't hear the rhythmic sound of the mop being pushed back and forth across the floor's hard surface. *Suppose I was confined to a wheelchair, and I wasn't strong enough to stand upright and grasp the wooden handle to erase the muddy footprints and make the floor shiny and clean again? Suppose I didn't have a home or a family to clean up after?*

When I thought about all these blessings, my grumbling turned into a prayer of thanksgiving. Thank You, Lord, for the privilege of mopping this dirty floor. Thank You for the health and the strength to hold this mop, for the ability to wrap my agile fingers around its handle and feel the wood in my hands. Thank You for the sight to see the crumbs and the dirt, for the sense of smell to enjoy the clean scent of the soap in my bucket. Thank You for the many precious feet that will walk through this room and dirty it again. Those feet are the reason I do this job. And Lord, thank You for the privilege of having a floor to mop and a family to clean up after.

Reptiles and Rodents

One muggy June morning, Steve and I held hands at the kitchen table for a quick prayer before he hurried off to work.

"Lord, we thank you for this beautiful summer day," Steve prayed. "I ask that Steven and Sharon will see and experience your creation in a new and fresh way today. Amen."

Summer is a wonderful time of year to experience God's creation, so Steve's prayer for my son and I was most welcome. Much to my horror and my son's delight, we have a plethora of color-changing, eyeball-blinking, tongue-hurling lizards around the perimeter of our house and yard. I decided years ago that I did not like anything that looked you in the eye and stuck out its tongue. However, if the lizards remain outside where God created them to live, and we don't have to make eye contact, I can ignore them completely. But on this particular day, Mr. Lizard invaded my kitchen.

Steven was nowhere to be found when I detected the lizard staring me in the face, so it was up to me to deal with this miniature dinosaur. A nearby broom was my weapon of choice. With my first swat, the lizard's tail promptly detached from its scaly body and lay dormant on the floor while the rest of him scurried across the room. More desperate swats followed. In the end, I won the battle, and the lizard was swept away . . . so to speak.

That afternoon, as I walked by my porch side door to the laundry room, I glanced out the window to see a huge black snake basking in the summer sun by the sidewalk steps. His head was erect and searching the area like a radar antenna. A frantic call to two neighborhood men, who were home for lunch, brought hoes, shovels, and excited children to witness the demise of the slithering reptile.

Emotionally weary from "seeing God's creation in a new and fresh way," that evening, I plopped down at the dinner table, staring out at our peaceful lawn. "What's that hopping across the yard?" I asked.

Steve stood up and watched a huge field mouse bound toward the area where our dog, Ginger, was sleeping. Alert to the scent, Ginger looked as though she wasn't quite sure what was expected of her, but she knew it was something. *Where's a snake when you need him,* I thought to myself. With the soft bite of a retriever, Ginger pawed and terrorized the misplaced rodent until my husband had no other choice but to put it out of its misery. By the time we dealt with Ginger's catch of the day, dinner was ruined.

One simple prayer, "Let Steven and Sharon see your creation in a new and fresh way," and what did we get? A lizard with a detachable tail in my kitchen, a black snake on my steps, and a field mouse for dinner entertainment. Psalm 5:3 NIV says, "In the morning I lay my requests before you and wait in expectation."

"Next time," I told my husband, "please be a little more specific in your prayers for our day."

Squawking or Chirping?

From May to August, my place for morning sustenance moves from the walnut barley-twist table of the kitchen to the black wrought-iron table on the patio. That's where I settled down one cool, summer morning with a fresh cup of piping hot coffee and my Bible, ready to spend some quality time with God. My flower gardens were at their peak, bursting with fuchsia, red, and white impatiens, begonias, and blue ageratum. The hanging baskets next to my patio chair were heavy with purple and pink velvet petunias, filling the air with a sweet fragrance not found in the finest department stores. It was one of those perfect, peaceful, storybook mornings.

I sat down close enough to the hanging baskets to keep the scent of the petunias wafting past my nose.

Suddenly, a little finch darted from the flower basket that had become his summer residence. He perched on a tree in front of me, furious that I had invaded his space, and angrily squawked in my direction. His mate perched beside him and sang a lovely song, but there was no calming down her "man." He hopped from the tree, to the chair, to the wall, to the table. With ruffled feathers and pointing his beak in my direction, he squawked at me to move. So much for quiet time. Finally, after forty-five minutes of this constant badgering, I could take it no longer and decided to give this bird a piece of my mind.

"Look buddy," I said aloud, "who planted those flower baskets in the first place? I did! Who hung and fertilized them? I did! And who waters them daily? I do! Don't you come out here complaining to me because I choose to sit here and enjoy what I've planted! They're mine in the first place—not yours. I'm just letting you live here. And you should be thankful for that! Besides, you're making a terrible mess!"

The more I reminded him of why he should be thankful and stop his complaining, the more he squawked. Trying to ignore the bird, I opened my Bible to Psalm 24:1-2, which read, "The earth is the LORD's and all it contains, the world, and those who dwell in it. For He has founded it upon the seas and established it upon the rivers."

Those angry squawks from the finch had a familiar ring. In fact, they sounded a lot like my own voice. Oh, how I complain when someone messes up my plans, when situations don't go my way, or when someone invades my space. My space. My plans. My way. My, my, my.

God's voice spoke to me from the pages of my Bible. *Who made this earth in the first place? Who has planted and watered all you have before you? I knew your days before you were even born. I've mapped them out. This whole earth is Mine and all that it contains. I'm just letting you live here. And besides, sometimes you make a terrible mess. Stop your squawking and start to chirp that song that I've put into your heart.*

In my quiet time, God had delivered His message loud and clear. My little feathered friend had shown me just how irritating my squawking could be.

Which Character Will You Play?

Sitting on a shelf in my kitchen are a variety of cookbooks packed with scrumptious recipes. But just because Betty Crocker and Martha Stewart are perched on my bookcase doesn't make me a gourmet cook. It's not until I take the book off the shelf and follow the directions in the recipe that the truth is revealed.

One Saturday night, my family hunkered down on a worn, den sofa with an oversized bowl of popcorn, tall glasses of soda, and an action-packed video: *Raider's of the Lost Ark,* starring Harrison Ford. We were ready to be entertained by suspense, intrigue, and a touch of romance. Like any good movie, there were three principal characters: the good guy, the bad guy, and the damsel in distress. The good guy, Dr. Indiana Jones, who was a professor of archeology, obtainer of rare antiquities, and student of the world-renowned Dr. Ravenwood of the University of Chicago, quickly charmed us. We were appalled by the bad guy, a waxy-faced Nazi with a sinister grin and breathy laugh, who was always accompanied by an entourage of brutal, salivating, gargantuan henchmen. Then there was the damsel in distress—the not so fair Marian, daughter of the now deceased Dr. Ravenwood and sole proprietor of a drinking establishment in the snowy mountains of Nepal.

In the opening scene, Dr. Jones is pulled from teaching his archeology class to meet with two agents from U.S. Army Intelligence. It seems that Hitler is obsessed with religion and the occult and is on a mission to find the whereabouts of the Ark of the Covenant which has been missing since Solomon's temple was destroyed in 586 B.C. Obviously, the government officials missed a few days in Sunday school, so Dr. Jones fills them in on the significance of the ark, that it contains *the* Ten Commandments and symbolizes the presence of God.

The government officials reveal that they have intercepted a German communication that reveals the Nazis are searching for the ark in Cairo, but in order to determine its exact location, they need a map that is engraved on a gold medallion, once owned by Dr. Ravenwood. Dr. Jones' mission, should he choose to accept it, is to locate the medallion, uncover the Ark of the Covenant, and bring it safely back to the United States.

Professor Jones removes his bow tie and wire-rim glasses and trades them for his suede hat, leather whip, and trusty pistol. Off he goes to Nepal to find the fair Marian and, hopefully, the medallion (which she has been wearing on a chain around her neck for years). Unfortunately for Marian, the waxy-faced Nazi also realizes that she is the key to finding the map and pays her a little visit. In adventure film fashion, a fight ensues, a fire breaks out, and the damsel's life is in peril. Just before the blazing walls come crashing down, the spy notices the golden medallion engulfed in flames, hanging from a pole. He grasps the metal disc from the flames, only to quickly drop it from his hot little hand, but not before it leaves a lasting impression. One side of the map is forever burned into the palm of his hand. Of course, Indiana comes to the rescue. The music soars, the hero cracks his whip, saves the damsel in distress, and recovers the medallion.

The Germans, thinking they have the map in the palm of their hand (actually in the palm of Mr. Waxy-face's hand) start to dig. But what Professor Jones realizes is that the map is on the front *and* the back of the medallion. The Germans have just half of the directions and are actually digging in the wrong place.

Now before I lose you altogether with this movie plot, I have to tell you that the Lord took what was supposed to be a mindless night of relaxation and entertainment and brought to light an invaluable lesson about searching for treasure. Many people want to discover spiritual treasure. Many people would like to have the presence of God in their camp. And just like in the movie, we could potentially play one of three roles.

Some people are like the damsel, who had been wearing the treasure map around her neck for years but had no idea what it was. She only wore it because her beloved father had given it to her as a gift. Likewise, there are those who wear a cross around their neck, but don't truly understand the significance of the gift from their Heavenly Father. There are others who have a dusty Bible on a crowded bookshelf or displayed on a living room coffee table, but don't realize that it contains the map to riches more valuable than silver or gold—the sustenance for life.

Some are like the bad guy with only one side of the medallion burned into the palm of his hand. They have heard parts of Scripture, read a few verses here and there, or have visited a church on holy days such as Easter or Christmas. They are searching for the hidden treasures of life, but because they don't understand the whole truth of God, they are digging in the wrong place.

Finally, some are like the heroic Dr. Jones, who possesses the whole map and knows exactly where to search for the treasure above all treasures—the Ark of the Covenant—the presence of God. Oh, the joy that comes from following God's map . . . not just parts of it . . . but all of it. For when we do, it will lead us to heavenly treasures, the presence of God, and the sustenance for life.

The movie was over. The credits rolled across the screen. My popcorn bowl was empty, but my heart was full of gratitude to God, who has given each of us access to His presence. The map is available to each of us. Which character will you play?

Dear Lord,

Thank You that the same God, who showered the Israelites with manna from heaven and called ravens to bring food to the prophet Elijah, still brings sustenance to His children today. Thank You for being our Living Bread from heaven—The Bread of Life that takes away our spiritual hunger, fills our cups to overflowing, and gives eternal life to all who call on Your name.

We look forward to the day when we will feast at Your banqueting table in glory. Until then, we praise You at our own kitchen tables for being our Sustenance for life.

Amen.

The Family Room

Surrounded by Love

Now that you've been refreshed in my kitchen, let's step into the family room. You can learn volumes about a person by spending a few moments in their family room. Cherished books crowd sagging shelves, beloved faces smile from gold and silver picture frames on coffee tables, and collected treasures passed down from generation to generation rest on neatly arranged mantles. The family room is a museum of memories, reminding us that the greatest gift of all is God's love.

So settle down in an overstuffed armchair. I'll fluff up your pillows, stoke the fire, and show you a few of my favorite family mementos. And if you listen closely, you'll be able to hear echoes of the past and sense the warmth of His presence in a room surrounded by love.

Grandma's Inheritance

One of the few black-and-white pictures resting on my mantle is of my father's mother. Grandma Edwards didn't have many material possessions, but she had a sharp mind, a determined spirit, and bucketsful of love. She was a small-framed woman who had raised a family of five children during the Depression by running a tiny general store and harvesting produce from her garden. As far back as I can remember, Grandma was always old. She wore her tightly braided ponytail wound around her head like a Swedish crown. I was always amazed to see the gray rope unfold down her back and stop at her waist when she took her hairpins out at night.

Another thing that always amazed me was Grandma's undergarments. She wore knit, baggy underwear that hung down to her knees and an equally attractive tee shirt to match. I never saw these undergarments anywhere except on Grandma's clothesline, so at the age of six, I decided that there must be a special old people's store that sold baggy underwear just for grandparents.

Grandma never owned a car. She never had a driver's license. When she needed groceries, she simply telephoned the local store and read the list that she had written on a scrap of brown paper bag, and a few hours later, a young boy would magically appear with her goods in a cardboard box. Grandma's house was filled with the aroma of strong coffee and freshly baked biscuits. There was also the scent of Suave, which was the all-time cure for any ailment, and of snuff, which she would sneak between her cheek and gum when she thought I wasn't looking.

I would spend a week at Grandma's house every summer. The highlight of our day was watching Perry Mason on her big black-and-white television. We drank Coca-Cola from cold, glass bottles and ate peanut butter crackers. Grandma had a standing date with Perry from three to four o'clock each day. If someone "came-a-callin'" during that time, they knew to pull up a chair, grab a Coke, and wait until the verdict was in before the conversation could begin.

During my weeks with her, there were no trips to fast-food restaurants or amusement parks, and no shopping sprees or excursions to the movies. That's just not what grandmas were for. So what did I do for seven days? I did what Grandma did. I made biscuits, shelled lima beans, canned vegetables for the following winter, and learned how to sew.

When I was six years old, Grandma taught me how to turn a square piece of daisy-covered cloth into a gathered apron with a big bow in the back. At seven, I learned how to turn a hot-pink, rectangular piece of cotton into a jumper with big ball buttons on the straps. At eight, we conquered the zipper.

Grandma didn't leave me a large sum of money when she passed away. But what she left me was much more valuable. Her inheritance was the peace that comes from leading a simple life and the joy that comes from creating things with my hands. If she could see me now, I'm not sure what she would think of my sewing machine with seventy-two stitches and a computer memory. But I'm sure she would smile as I'd say, "Look, Grandma, I made all these curtains and pillows. And look Grandma, how do you like my dress I whipped up? See the zipper? I didn't even have to rip it out and start over once this time."

Without realizing it, my grandmother modeled a Titus 2 woman for me: "Older women . . . encourage the young women to love their husbands, to love their children, to be sensible, pure, workers at home . . ." (Titus 2:3-5). And she taught me how to be a Proverbs 31 woman who works with her hands in delight, brings her food from afar, clothes her household with scarlet, makes coverings for herself and belts for the tradesmen, and does not eat the bread of idleness.

Leaving an inheritance to our children is so much more than money in the bank, well-invested mutual funds, and heirlooms of silver and jewels. It is leaving them memories of simple times together, instructing them on how to become men and women of God, and leaving a legacy which causes them to "rise up and call you blessed."

A Little Child Shall Lead Them

As the happy faces of our little Jaynes' threesome smile back at me from various pictures around our family room, I'm reminded that God's plans and our plans are not always the same.

My son, Steven, was two years old when my husband and I decided it was time to give him a little brother or sister. Steven was conceived with no problem whatsoever, so we thought this would be a great opportunity to build a little faith in our son. We sat him down one night and explained, "Steven, Mommy and Daddy want you to have a little brother or sister. But it's God who blesses parents with children, so we are going to pray that He will bless us with another baby."

That sounded like a pretty good idea to Steven, so we made our request a part of our family prayer time each night and always closed with, "And Lord, please give Mommy and Daddy another baby. Amen."

By the time Steven was three years old, we still didn't have any news of an impending sibling. But we continued to pray faithfully. I was afraid that Steven was going to think, "And Lord, please give Mommy and Daddy another baby" was a doxology, or something that you say before the "Amen" at the end of every prayer.

By age four, we still had no news for Steven. I was really starting to worry about how this "unanswered prayer" was going to affect his faith and wanted to get out of this gracefully. Obviously, it was not the Lord's desire for us to have another child at this time, but I didn't know how to tell Steven that we didn't have to pray that prayer *every* night. I kept hoping that he would just forget about it. But he didn't forget about it any more than he forgot the "Amen" at the end of a prayer.

So I began to pray, "Lord, please show me how to ease out of this predicament. Show me how to get Steven to stop praying for another baby and how to get him to just forget about it."

We had a miniature table and chairs in the kitchen where Steven and I ate lunch together each day. One day, Steven looked up, and in his sweet little voice said, "Mommy, did you ever think that maybe God only wants you to have one child?"

After I picked myself up from the floor, I answered, "Yes, I have thought that maybe that is the case and if it is, I am so thankful because He has given me all I have ever hoped for in a child wrapped up in one package, YOU!"

Then he turned his little head like a robin and said, "But I think what we ought to do is keep praying until you're too old to have one. Then we'll know that's His answer."

What a great idea! The Lord had spoken to this child and used him to minister to his mother.

A favorite song Steven used to sing when he was four was: "My God is so big, so strong, and so mighty. There's nothing my God cannot do. The mountains are His. The valleys are His. The stars are His handiwork, too. My God is so big, so strong, and so mighty. There's nothing my God cannot do."

Steven didn't know how old "too old" was, but he did know that God *could* do anything. If God's answer was "no," Steven didn't have a problem with it. After all, I told him "no" many times, and he understood that "no" did not mean, "I don't love you." "No" just meant "no," because I said so, and because I know what's best for him. I was the one whose faith was being challenged by the possibility of this prayer not being answered as I wanted it to be.

The Lord taught me a great lesson that day. Through Steven's childlike faith, God gave me an example of the attitude of trust that I should have toward my Heavenly Father, who loves me and knows what's best for me.

Dear Mommy

Sometimes when I gaze at the Jaynes' family portraits of three smiling faces, I can almost see the shadow of a fourth, for there are four of us, and one day our picture will be complete.

"Steve, can you meet me for lunch?" I was so excited to share some unexpected news with my husband that I called him at the office and asked him to meet me at our favorite spot for lunch. "I have a little surprise I want to give you," I said.

After years of infertility treatments, we had become content with the realization that it must be God's desire for our son, Steven, to be raised as an only child. And now, this surprise!

At lunch, as Steve opened the tiny package containing a baby pillow wrapped in soft white tissue, he asked, "Does this mean what I think it means?"

We both blinked back tears, and all I could manage was a nod that said, "Yes, I'm pregnant."

After five long years of trying to conceive, the Lord had blessed us with this unexpected pregnancy. But our elation was soon changed to sadness when the pregnancy ended in a miscarriage two months later. For those of us who believe that life begins at conception, a miscarriage can be devastating, because it is not simply the loss of a child who is to be; it is the loss of a child who *is.*

One summer night a few months after the miscarriage as I lay on my bed, crying and praying, I wondered, *What is my daughter doing in heaven? What does she look like?* If only I could see a glimpse of her face or have one conversation with her. I felt as though the light of my life was being snuffed out by unbearable grief. With a miscarriage, there is no funeral—no sympathy cards. I needed closure. Then God reached down and gave me a precious gift that lit up my darkened soul and set my whole being aglow with His love. Just as clearly as if I were reading words on a printed page, a letter was spoken to my heart. When the words stopped coming, I jumped up and wrote them down. I hope that by sharing these words, I will give comfort and hope to those who have experienced the pain of empty arms.

Dear Mommy,

I asked Jesus if it would be all right for me to write you a letter. He said it would be OK.

First of all, I want to thank you for loving me and giving me life. I remember how happy you and Daddy were when you found out that you were going to have me. I remember how you prayed that I would come to know Christ at an early age. I remember how you prayed that I would have a mission in life to help others.

Mom, I know that you and Dad were sad when God decided to take me to heaven before I was born. I saw the tears that you cried. But Mom, what I wanted to tell you is this. Your prayers were answered. I am healthy. I am strong. I do know Christ, and He lets me sit on His lap everyday. And Mom, I do have a mission. Every day new babies come to heaven who were never born. Many of them never knew the love of a mother or father. These babies were removed from their mothers by human hands, not God's hands. When they come to heaven, they always ask the same question; "Baby Jaynes, tell me, what was it like to have the love of a mother?" And I can tell them. Oh, how I can tell them.

Thank you, Mom, for loving me. I know you miss me. But one day we will be together and what a time we will have. Until then, imagine me happy and whole, playing at the feet of Jesus, and telling other babies about what it feels like to have a mommy that loves them.

See you soon,
Baby Jaynes

What a precious gift the Lord had given me! The time of mourning had passed. I still have days when I long for this child. Some days when I look at portraits of our threesome on the family room walls, I almost see a fourth shadow in the sunlight. But there will come a day when my little girl will not be a mere shadow. I will hold her in my arms. Until then, it gives me great comfort to picture her as healthy and whole and being held lovingly in the arms of Christ.

Putting on the Dog

Over our walnut-paneled mantle hangs a portrait of a six-year-old Steven and the canine member of our clan, Ginger. Just as God has taught me a few lessons through my child, He also has shed light on a few areas through our dog.

Our golden retriever has quite a reputation for barking at anyone who dares to come up our driveway or sidewalk. But mostly, she barks at little old ladies and innocent young children. Most of the time when she barks, her tail is wagging at the same time, which makes her a little less convincing. But occasionally, she'll make the hair on her back stand up in an effort to look the part of a ferocious guard dog.

Our friends have learned that if they say, "Hi, Ginger," she immediately stops barking, tucks her tail between her legs, and rolls over on her back in submission. Even though I knew she was a virtual wimp and one of the most cowardly dogs I have ever known, I still considered her somewhat of a deterrent against unwanted solicitors and would-be robbers. Boy, was I disappointed when a neighbor informed me that Ginger only barks when we're at home! When we're gone, she doesn't even bother to stand up, much less growl. One day someone walked right by her, entered our garage, and stole a leaf blower . . . with her blessing, I'm sure.

One spring we hired a man to paint the outside of our house. He came while I was away and had been painting all day. That afternoon when I arrived home, I was greeted with a picture of tranquillity; the painter was standing on the ladder with Ginger lying peacefully at his feet. When I drove up the driveway, Ginger jumped up from her rest and went into action, barking at her friend the painter like there was no tomorrow.

"What's she doing?" he asked. "That's the first peep I've heard from her all day!"

Seven years later, Ginger still only performs when her masters can see her. It has made me stop and think. How many times have I performed correctly just because someone was watching me? The thing is, my Master is always looking, and I shouldn't just "put on the dog" when it appears I'm being watched.

Lassie Come Home

Ginger has not been the only dog in my life. My prize possession when I was eight years old was a collie dog named, what else, Lassie. Lassie was my shadow. She ran alongside me as I pedaled around the neighborhood on my pink-glittered banana bike. She slept outside the door of my one-room playhouse when my best friend, Wanda, and I "camped out." She protected me from dangerous strangers, such as the paperboy, the mailman, and the trash collector.

When the veterinarian told us that Lassie had an incurable skin disease and needed to be put to sleep, I was devastated. And even though she was my dog, my dad was almost as heartbroken as I was. He could not bring himself to end Lassie's life on purpose, so he drove her out to an old farmhouse about fifteen miles from town.

"Could you please take care of my dog for me?" he asked the old farmer. "She's got a skin disease, but I can't bring myself to put her down."

"Sure," the fellow agreed. "Just leave her here. We'll look after her for you."

I never did get the particulars. Did he pay the man? Was he a nice man? Did he have children? All I knew was that Dad had done the best he could.

Months later, Dad went by to check in on the old girl. "I'm sorry, Mr. Edwards," the old farmer said. "Lassie ran away a few days after you left her here. We've never seen her since."

Dad never told me Lassie had run away. But each time he drove into Tarboro, the town near where he had left her, he panned the landscape, looking for a lost dog that answered to the name of Lassie.

Miraculously, one day he spotted a collie wandering around the street. Dad jumped out of his car, pulled his pipe out of his mouth, and called out, "Lassie, here girl. Come here, girl." As he clapped his hands together, the dog bounded toward my dad, almost knocking him off his feet. A flurry of fur, tail wagging, and sloppy dog kisses smothered Dad as the two were reunited. What a surprise we had that evening when Lassie came cruising home in the gray Buick.

"Lassie! Lassie!" I cried.

I had never seen such a welcome sight. As a matter of fact, her skin disease was completely gone, and her coat was thicker and more beautiful than ever. All was well with the world.

Two weeks later, my older brother was out wrestling with Lassie in the yard. Dazed and ashen faced, he stumbled through the door.

"Mom, we've got a big problem," he said. "You know, Lassie, well . . . well . . . she's not a lassie at all. She's a laddie. This dog is a boy!"

"What!" my mother exclaimed.

We ran outside and rolled Lassie (Laddie) over on her (his) back. And there it was. She was a he, and this was not our dog! No wonder her (his) coat looked so thick and healthy.

"Mom," I said, "if this isn't Lassie, then who is it! We've stolen someone's pet!"

Needless to say, we put ads in the Tarboro and Rocky Mount papers, but no one ever claimed Laddie. He seemed perfectly content at our home, so there he stayed.

Have you ever wanted something so badly—hunted, searched, and maybe even prayed—then when you found it, you realized that maybe it wasn't exactly what you wanted, but it was definitely what you needed? I wanted my dog back. Laddie wanted a family. And for one little girl and a stray pup, God answered my prayer. As usual, His answer had an unexpected twist, but it was perfect in every way.

Nightmare on York Street

There is one object in my family room that I would just assume not be there—the television. But it appears it's here to stay. Growing up, our family room also had a television, but I didn't like it much back then either.

One night when I was thirteen, I laid in my bed, unmoving, wide-eyed, and paralyzed by fear after watching a scary movie with my dad. The silence was interrupted only by the sound of my heart, drumming in my ears. The movie, *In Cold Blood,* about two murderous maniacs and their race from the law, littered the screen with a trail of heinous crimes as the crazed men traversed the countryside. By today's standards, this movie would be considered mild. But to this thirteen-year-old girl, it was the scariest thing I had ever seen.

So as I lay quivering in my bed with the covers clinched tightly against my chin, I fully expected the two killers to make my house at 725 York Street their next stop. The fact that my dad was asleep in the next room was no comfort whatsoever. At some point, my mother made her way to their room. I heard her open their bedroom door. I heard her steps as she walked toward their bed. Then suddenly, I heard a man let out a blood-curdling scream and what sounded like my mother being thrown against the wall with a thud.

"Get out! Get out!" she shrieked.

I bolted upright in the bed and knew I had to escape before the killers made their way to my room. Straining to open the window, I finally managed to push it up and jump out onto the wet grass. Clambering to my feet, I tried to run toward my neighbor's house. My mind was racing faster than my shaking legs, and several times I tumbled to the ground. As if in slow motion, I ran, tripped, and crawled to Mrs. Dixon's house.

Bam! Bam! Bam! I pounded on the wooden door. No answer. Bam! Bam! Bam!

The household awoke, and lights sprang to life. Mrs. Dixon cautiously cracked the door to find a trembling teenager with a mixture of white night cream and mud smeared on her face, hair pulled up in a rubber band

and wound around one gargantuan curler, bare wet feet, and tattered pajamas.

"Good Lord, Sharon. What has happened to you?" she exclaimed as she pulled me in out of the cold. Between sobs, I described the scene (in graphic detail, I might add). "There's a bloodthirsty murderer in my house. He has already killed my father and now he's killing my mom! I jumped out the window to escape! You've got to help us!" I pleaded as I grabbed at her robe.

By now, the entire Dixon household was awake and had gathered in the den. Included in my audience was their handsome son, five years my senior, whom I was always desiring to impress. Before notifying the police, Mrs. Dixon decided to call my home. Surprisingly, my mom answered.

"Louise, this is Margarite. Sharon is over here and says someone's trying to kill you. Are you all right?"

My mom, who had no idea I had fled the premises, explained, "There's no problem over here. Allan watched a scary movie on TV tonight. He had a nightmare that a murderer was coming after him. Right when I crawled into bed, he was dreaming the boogeyman was grabbing his shoulder. Allan jumped up and pushed me against the wall."

Listening in on my mom's response, I pleaded, "She's not telling the truth! He's making her say that. He's killed my dad, and he's holding her hostage. I heard her yell, 'Get out! Get out!'"

"No," Mom assured, "I yelled, 'Get the light! Get the light!'"

Somehow, Mom convinced the Dixons that no crime had been committed and it was safe for me to come home. Reluctantly, I made my way back across the yard (accompanied by the son whom I can safely say had been duly impressed). My mother was fine. However, my dad was looking through all the closets in the house with a flashlight.

I've never enjoyed scary movies since then and have concluded that being terrified out of my mind is not my idea of entertainment. And even though it may not be real, it can sure feel that way. Here's a little acronym I remember for fear: False Evidence Appearing Real. Yes, there is a real boogeyman. His name is Satan, and he seeks to kill, steal, and destroy (John 10:10). His weapon? Lies. He whispers lies. He wants us to worry about things that are not real. He desires to steal our peace, rob our sleep, stir up doubt, and distort what we hear. He twists the truth and plunders our thoughts. His goal is to make us jump, run, or be paralyzed into inactivity. Oh, he's real all right. But his lies are not. It's just false evidence appearing real.

I suggest you do a little FBI work of your own (Further Bible Investigation). Dust for fingerprints on the worries of your life. I bet they have Satan's fingerprints all over them.

By the way, there's already a warrant out for his arrest. Right now he's out on parole. But this is one movie where I've already seen the ending. Satan gets his due. The list of credits is short—there's only one name—Jesus.

As my mom yelled, "Get the Light! Get the Light!"

Who's the Boss?

Some pictures in my family room are of those who were a part of our household, if only for a short time. One such photo is of a Russian foreign-exchange student, who lived with us for a few months.

One spring when my son was in the fourth grade, we invited a ten-year-old foreign-exchange student to stay in our home and attend Charlotte Christian School with Steven. As soon as Andre* walked off the plane and into our lives, it became apparent that this was more than a foreign exchange experience for him. He was on vacation . . . from authority—*all* authority.

I suspect Andre's comprehension of the English language was a lot better than he let on. Even though his command of the language was tentative, his command of the word "no" was profound. When I made a request, such as, "Andre, put on your jacket," he would look me in the eye and say, "No." I calmly continued to repeat the request, "Andre, put on your jacket," with his repeating "No," until one of us became tired. It was never me. My favorite line was, "In America, parents are the boss."

My requests were never unreasonable, but one particular request met with great opposition every time. It was, "Andre, it's time to take a bath." Once, however, Andre did comply with the bath-time request without one single argument. *Now we're getting somewhere,* I thought. After he ran the bath water, I walked by the bathroom to check on him, only to find him standing next to the bathtub, fully clothed, waiting for the proper amount of time to pass before letting the water out. What a lot of trouble to go through just to avoid a bath!

Steven had always been a fairly compliant child. However, at age two, his favorite word was also "no." But by age three, he had learned that, "In America, parents are the boss." So this strong will in Andre was new to me, but I was up for the challenge and did not waver.

The two months passed. Andre got back on the plane with new clothes, new shoes, and other new American merchandise. I'm not sure how much he learned from the American Christian experience. I didn't feel like it was much. But I learned a lot about the word "no."

When a two-year-old child looks you in the eye and puckers up his sweet little cherry lips to form the word "no," sometimes it can be kind of cute. However, when a ten-year-old looks you straight in the eye and unabashedly forms that same word, it's not cute any longer. How must the Lord feel when we plant our feet, with hands on our hips, and say no to Him? Yet God just continues repeating Himself until one of us gets tired. And guess what? It's never Him.

Have you figured out who's the Boss in your life? If not, He is patient enough to work with you until you figure it out.

Not his real name.

From Diaper Cream to Acne Cream

One of the most moving experiences for an empty nester is flipping through the pages of photo albums and reminiscing about the years of parenting that seemed to fly by so quickly. There's the picture of the newborn with the squinted, rosy face in his hospital bassinet. Then in the twinkling of an eye, that same child is standing in cap and gown at his high school graduation. There's the little princess at her preschool ballet recital, and just a few pages over, a young bride stands at the altar in a lacy wedding gown. And as the children grow and change, mothers are expected to grow and change with them, snipping the apron strings along the way.

The year my son turned twelve held many traumatic changes (for his mother, that is). He started middle school, which meant changing classes, but I didn't realize that so many other things would change as well. His voice dropped an octave, the smell of the laundry took a definite turn for the worse, and his five-foot-seven-inch frame passed my five-foot-five. For the first time since kindergarten, Steven told me that it really wasn't necessary for me to drive on one of his class field trips. That translates, "I'd rather you not go, Mom." I was crushed but determined not to make him feel guilty about his growing need for independence.

Then there was the swing set. When Steven was three years old, my husband built an awesome wooden swing set with two swings, a trapeze bar, a slide, and a two-story fort. For several years, I would squeeze through the door of the upper level of the fort where Steven and I ate many lunches together. Of course, we never ate in the lower level, because that was the jail, and as he explained, "Nobody wants to eat in a jail."

At age twelve, Steven enlightened me with some facts about the beloved swing set. "Mom, that swing set hasn't seen much action in the past year. As a matter of fact, I can't even fit through the fort doors anymore. I think we need to take it down."

"Take it down! You must be kidding," I said defensively. "Of course you can still fit through the doors. I still fit just fine."

Then it hit me as he answered, "Yeah, Mom, but now I'm a lot bigger than you."

So we took a family vote, and I lost two to one. The shrine to Steven's childhood came down, and a gazebo was erected in its place.

Another heavy blow fell at breakfast one morning when Steven looked up and sheepishly stated, "Mom, Monday is Rosemary's birthday."

Rosemary was a cute girl in Steven's class that he had mentioned from time to time. Knowing there was more to this story, I said, "And?"

"And I'd like to get her a little something. I'll use my own money."

This was hard to take, knowing that I was now not the only girl in Steven's life. But without flinching, I took him to a gift shop and helped him pick out "a little something."

As Steven moved toward adulthood, my prayer was that he would increasingly depend on the Lord as he gained independence from us. Cutting those apron strings was difficult. However, I knew that if I didn't keep those scissors sharp and clip them gradually when it was time, they'd be ripped out later.

As I prayed about all the changes in Steven's life that seemed to be coming far too fast, the Holy Spirit reminded me of another mother who faced many changes as her Son turned twelve. I think it was probably a traumatic time for Mary. She and Joseph had taken Jesus on a journey to Jerusalem to celebrate the Passover. On their way back home, they noticed that He was missing. They frantically searched the caravan, only to come up empty-handed. Finally, three days later, they found Jesus back in the Jerusalem temple, listening and asking questions of his teachers.

If we had been there, and if Mary had worn an apron, we probably could have heard a snip. What a privilege it was for Mary to be the earthly mother of Jesus, even though it was only for a short time. And what a privilege it has been for me to be the mother of a precious son, also knowing that he is God's gift to me for a short season. All mothers have to learn how to let go of their children. It doesn't come naturally. But when we realize that they are merely moving from our arms to the Father's, the transition can be sweet and the apron strings a little easier to snip.

The Gift

One of the most treasured heirlooms on any family-room bookshelf is the wedding album. Their wedding day is the one time in a couple's life when all the people they love surround them at the same time. Many of the gifts they receive touch their lives in a deep and lasting way.

Bridal showers are so predictable. Mounds of various sized boxes are wrapped in shiny silver and glossy-white paper, topped with beautifully crafted bows. Toaster ovens, electric can openers, stainless steel mixing bowls, everyday dishes, and fine china are the gifts of choice. Compliments echo around the room as each treasure is carefully unwrapped and passed around for inspection. The choir of onlookers, who have traveled this road years before, offer useful advice and comments like,

"You'll need that," or "I still use my stainless bowls that I got for a wedding present back in '55," or "You can never have too many pot holders." And so it goes.

My bridal shower was no exception. However, one present stood out above all the crock-pots, bath towels, and silverware. It was a gift from my mother, Louise Anderson Edwards.

In 1956, my mother discovered she was pregnant with me, her second child. To pass the time, this twenty-four-year-old woman decided to learn how to crochet. Her mother-in-law, a magician with needle and thread, taught Louise the ins and outs of the craft.

My mother was one of twelve children, raised on a tobacco farm in Nash County, North Carolina. She didn't know a lot about the fine gauge of one hundred percent wool skeins of yarn. But she knew about the strength and durability of one hundred percent cotton household twine. In her youth, my mother used household twine, which she knew as "tobacco twine," to tie up bundles of the huge, green-tobacco leaves before hanging them from the barn rafters to dry.

It was this same twine that my mother's nimble fingers used to crochet a beautiful bedspread for the new child she was carrying. Love was woven into the spread with each stitch that her mind silently counted.

The project took eight months to complete. I was born just as the last of the fringed border was tatted into place.

Too soon, I outgrew my crib and was ready for my first bed. But it wasn't the masterpiece Mom had created that graced my bed. Instead, ballerinas in airy, white-and-pink tutus danced across the fabric of my bedspread and on the canopy over my head. The crocheted bedspread was buried away like a treasure to be discovered twenty-three years later.

At my bridal shower, everyone crowded around to see what grand finale my mom had saved as the last gift to be opened. I carefully unwrapped the package and plucked the bow from its lid. As I removed the top and folded back layers of tissue paper, I saw the beautiful crocheted bedspread that my mother had created while God was creating me.

"You can never have too many bedspreads," commented one of the old-timers.

"And you can never have too much love," I echoed.

Four years later, as God was knitting together my first child in my womb, I took up quilting. My first project took eight months to complete, and love was woven into each tiny stitch. I have visions of one day taking this quilt to my future daughter-in-law's bridal

shower. Then among the gifts of pots and pans, she'll open the beautifully wrapped box.

Someone will say, "You can never have too many quilts."

And I will echo, "And you can never have too much love."

The Wonder of You: To Steven from Mom

Of all the pictures that crowd a family-room shelf, it is perhaps the ones of our children that we cherish the most. Their smiling faces chronicle a love that grows sweeter and more precious with every passing year. Each stage of a child's life brings new challenges and new joys—each a magnificent wonder and a gift.

As parents, we give our children roots; then we give them wings. But the most frightening parental experience is when we give them wheels. The following is a letter that I wrote to my son on the morning I took him to get his driver's permit. The images may change, but the wonder of a child remains constant and eternal.

I crept into your room today as the sun peeked over the horizon. A single ray of light reached through the blinds and illuminated your angelic face like a lone actor on a stage. Two tiny fists framed your olive face as you snuggled peacefully under your yellow blanket.

A small head, capped with black, bushy hair. Long Bambi-like eyelashes. Perfectly formed cherub lips. A red forceps mark on your forehead. Knees curled and tucked under your tummy. A mound of love that just three days before kicked my ribs and moved inside my tummy, now slept in a tiny crib and moved my heart.

Yellow-gingham bumper pads framed this picture of sweetness, tranquility, and love. I drank in the scent of baby powder, fresh wipes, and lotion.

A Noah's Ark soft-sculpted toy with ten bulging pockets carried animals two-by-two. A bunny-shaped rattle waited for a tiny hand. A tinkling music box was silent. Stuffed animals with bright satin bows huddled in a corner. A white-wicker rocker beckoned me to rock you.

I stroked your head and watched you breathe, finding my chest in sync with yours. You are my precious gift from God, I thought. What journeys await our family of three? I crept into your room today and thanked God for the wonder of you.

I crept into your room today before you awoke. In a few short moments, you'd be calling out in your two-year-old voice for mommy and daddy to lift you out of your now too small crib for a little snuggle time before dad went off to work.

Your black hair has been replaced with golden corn silk, capping your precious head. Long thick eyelashes, now dubbed as "angel wings," rest on your chubby cheeks.

The yellow blanket that once kept you warm now keeps you secure as you clutch it tightly to your side. Somehow your thumb had found its way to your mouth, and I heard the sound of gentle sucking.

Big Bird and Ernie waited patiently for their little friend to stir. A train was parked in the corner. A stick horse was tethered to the doorknob. Rubber balls and wooden blocks were piled high in a basket. Pop-up books like Richard Scarey, Lowly Worm, Busy People, and Things that Go are all familiar friends crowded on the bookshelf. Wooden puzzles, plastic trucks, and cardboard tubes for jousting lay at your feet. A well-worn wicker rocker has become my favorite spot in the house.

I stroked your blond head and watched your gentle breathing, still amazed that so much love could be found in one small package. I crept into your room today and thanked God for the wonder of you.

I crept into your room today on your first day of school. In Superman pajamas, hugging a well-worn teddy bear, you dreamed of new friends and adventure.

A new shiny-red lunchbox sat on the dresser. Stiff new jeans and a crisp striped-knit shirt was laid out on the floor. A blue backpack stuffed with fresh crayons, markers, and wide-ruled notebook paper, hung from the doorknob. Plastic swords, play Indians, Nerf balls, a sheriff's badge, and cowboy boots would all be motionless this day. A T-Ball trophy dominated the dresser. A team picture of twelve miniature athletes smiled back at me from a red frame on the wall.

I stroked your sandy-blond head, and tears streamed down my cheeks. In just a few minutes, I'd walk you down a sidewalk and entrust my most valued possession into the hands of another woman. Would your teacher know that you were the most creative child that God had ever fashioned? Would she know that you already knew your ABC's and could count to a hundred? Would she know that you had already asked Jesus to come into your heart and could recite the Lord's Prayer and Twenty-third Psalm? Would she know that you needed lots of hugs? Would she know that this was one of the hardest days of my life?

Oh, how I would miss my little man today! I crept into your room today and thanked God for the wonder of you.

I crept into your room today before the sun made its way into the morning sky. You, my little soldier, lay tangled in the sheets, and Beary, the polar bear, who stared admiringly into his charge's tranquil face, was tucked under your arm.

The cars-and-trucks wallpaper had been replaced by plaids and coat-of-arms. Baseball hats hung from the corners of your four-poster bed. Soccer pictures lined the walls, and a Boy Scout handbook lay on the floor. Well-worn matchbox cars parked in a slotted carrying case. Stray Legos peeked from under the bed. G. I. Joes, back from their latest mission, shared a shelf with hard-to-part-with stuffed animals. A flashlight rested on *The Chronicles of Narnia.*

I stroked your head and wondered if you had any idea how much I have loved being your mom for these past ten years. I crept into your room today and thanked God for the wonder of you.

I crept into your room today before the day was new. Breaking all the new rules of privacy and personal space, I gazed at my twelve-year-old young man with a sense of awe.

A knowing Michael Jordan smiled at me from a poster taped on the closet door. Muddy baseball pants hung over a chair. Inverted tube socks were wadded up and tossed in a corner. A CD player, headphones, and magazines were stacked on the floor. Deodorant, boxer shorts, and fuzzy legs symbolize your growth. Five-feet nine-inches of muscle and bone: a man-child metamorphoses before my very eyes.

A school yearbook lay open to page eighty-seven; a certain girl's smiling face was the last thing on your mind before you went to sleep. A new era is on the horizon. I whispered a prayer of protection, purity, and purpose over your sleeping form as I rubbed your sandy head. I crept into your room today and thanked God for the wonder of you.

I crept into your room today before the alarm signaled the dawn of a new day. Your six-foot frame lay angled across the mattress. A man's hairy leg peeked out from under the tangled sheet. Your face needed a shave. A muscular arm hugged a willing pillow.

Your chubby cheeks and pug nose have been replaced with handsome angular lines, a strong jawbone, a determined nose, and a thick shock of unruly hair.

A geometry book leaned against the dresser. Ribbons and plaques from races proudly won hung from the floor-lamp arm. A rack of neckties and khaki pants mingled with tee shirts and jeans. A track-team warm-up suit was slung over a chair. A basketball letter and pin leaned against the mirror. An electric guitar, amplifier, distorter, and Christian-punk CDs dominated the room. A TARHEELS license plate rested on an easel, pointing to future dreams.

My little boy has become a man in the twinkling of an eye, in the flash of a moonbeam, in the time it takes a shooting star to traverse the night sky. I smoothed your thick hair and watched your chest rise and fall. What a gift you have been to me! How will I ever let you go? Today, I will drive you to the Department of Motor Vehicles to pick up your license to new freedoms. I will go as a driver, but return as a passenger.

A tear escaped my eye and trickled down my chin, as I was reminded once again that this chapter of my life is coming closer to an end. I crept into your room today and thanked God for the wonder of you.[1]

[1] Excerpted from *Being a Great Mom, Raising Great Kids* by Sharon Jaynes. (Chicago: Moody Press, 2000), pp. 247-250. Used by permission.

Dear Lord,

Thank You so much for creating this wonderful institution called the family. While I tend to skip over all the "begets" in Scripture, I realize that You put them in there because family is an important and vital part of Your plan.

Father, so many of Your children do not have happy childhood memories. Help us always remember that the family we came from is important but not as important as the one we leave behind.

Most of all, thank You for adopting those of us who have accepted Jesus Christ as Savior into Your family—the household of faith. Thank You for enfolding, disciplining, accepting, directing, nurturing, protecting, and comforting Your children. I love You, Lord, and rest in the assurance that because I am Your child, I am surrounded by love.

Amen.

Elise
2000

The Bedroom

Rest for the Weary

When I decorated my bedroom, I made sure it reflected a place of rest. A four-poster bed with a fluffy floral comforter and scattered ruffled pillows invites me to quiet my spirit and refresh my soul. A cozy wing chair and ottoman in the corner waits for me to relax and put my feet up with a much-loved book. This is my haven, my secret retreat, where I am refreshed, restored, and revitalized.

I'm so glad that rest was God's idea. It says in Genesis 2:12 that even He rested from the work of creation. The twenty-third Psalm says of the Shepherd: "He makes me lie down in green pastures; He leads me beside quiet waters. He restores my soul" (verses two and three).

Even though the demands of life scream and push at us to accomplish just one more goal or cross off one more task from our to-do list, the gentle coaxing of the Father woos us to come away by ourselves "to a secluded place and rest a while" (Mark 6:31).

Are you tired, stressed, and fatigued? If you are "tuckered out," come to the One who wants to tuck you in. Check your burdens at the door, and cease your striving. Let God sing you a lullaby and give you rest.

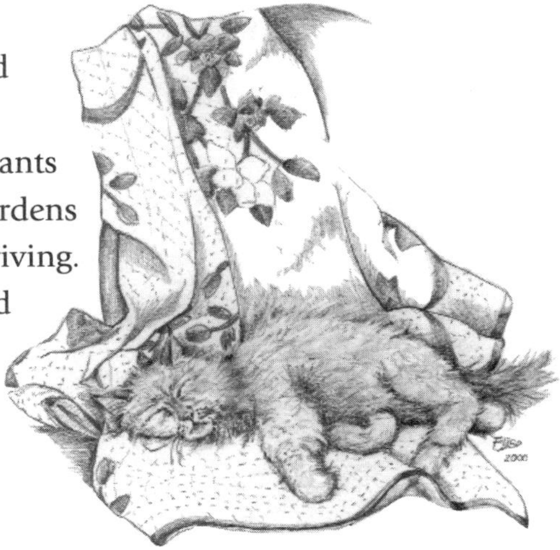

Mrs. Jaynes, You're Leading Again

Psalm 23:2 paints a tranquil picture of a shepherd leading his flock to rest and refreshment when it says, "He leads me beside quiet waters." But as one of God's sheep, the question is, will I follow Him there?

After ten years of marriage, I convinced my masculine husband to take a few ballroom dance classes with me. We had just read a book titled *His Needs Her Needs* by Willard Harley Jr. on how to have an excellent marriage. Harley suggests that couples spend about fifteen hours a week giving each other their undivided attention by communicating and sharing some recreational activity. Even though we already had an excellent marriage, we decided to take Harley's advice and find some activity that we would both enjoy doing together. Steve suggested golf. I suggested ballroom dancing. After one look at my potential golf swing, we ended up in a ballroom dance studio.

Steve and I had been to a resort in Sea Island, Georgia and had watched couples as they glided around the dance floor, dresses flowing, moving as one, to the fluid sounds of a professional orchestra playing music from the Big Band era. That's what I wanted to do! I wanted us to be Ginger Rogers and Fred Astaire. So I signed us up for ballroom dance classes, with visions of grandeur.

"Okay, Dr. and Mrs. Jaynes," the instructor began, "the first thing we will learn is a dance called the fox-trot. Dr. Jaynes, you place your right hand on your wife's left shoulder blade. Cup it firmly in your hand." Then she turned to me. "Now Mrs. Jaynes, you gently rest your left hand on your husband's right shoulder." So far so good, we all agreed.

She proceeded to teach us how to make little boxes with our feet while counting 1-2-3-4, 1-2-3-4. (Floating around the room as one, this was not.) The instructor smiled at Steve and said, "Dr. Jaynes, you have the hardest part because the man has to learn how to lead. All the woman has to do is follow." More than once she tapped me on the shoulder and said, "Mrs. Jaynes, you're leading again." The problem was, when I led, Steve wouldn't follow, and the train couldn't run with two engines.

I quickly became bored with the little boxes and asked, "Can we learn to move around the room a little instead of making boxes in the same spot all the time?" We then learned how to modify our box so it looked like a box with a flap open. We took two steps sideways and two steps backward. Actually, Steve got to move forward, and I had to move backward, which seemed totally unfair to me. I understood that we both could not move forward, but why did it have to be the woman who moved backward? The instructor assured me that this was the way God had planned it. I had wanted to feel like Ginger Rogers, gliding in graceful movements across the dance floor, but instead, I felt like a shopping buggy being pushed through the supermarket; and Steve looked more like Fred Rogers instead of Fred Astaire. All the while, I was being reprimanded: "Mrs. Jaynes, you're leading again."

We also had to learn not to look down at our feet, but at each other. "Concentrate on looking at each other's face," the instructor said. "Looking at your feet will not make them do the right steps. You just need to listen to the music and let your feet move you around the room."

Yeah, right, I thought. I felt better looking down, as if my eyes could will my feet into the correct steps.

Eventually however, I did learn to keep my eyes on my leader's handsome face.

After our first forty-five minute class was over, the instructor warned, "Now you must go home and practice. If you don't practice, it won't take long to forget everything you learned today." Let's just say, she was right.

So it goes. Sometimes it's not fun to learn those fundamental but necessary beginning steps of our walk with God. We want to glide through our spiritual journey with ease and beauty, moving effortlessly across life's dance floor. By learning those basic first steps and through continued practice, we can avoid stepping on everyone's toes and tripping over our own feet. Hebrews 5:14 states, "Solid food is for the mature, who because of practice have their senses trained to discern good and evil."

Don't worry. God knows all the steps, and He's a great Leader. That's where the resting comes in. We just need to place our hands gently on His shoulder, let Him lead, and focus on our Leader's face rather than our own "feats." I'm so thankful for the Holy Spirit who continues to tap me on the shoulder and says, "Mrs. Jaynes, you're leading again."

Trick Skis

Some nights I march straight to my bed, collapse on top of the covers, and fall asleep before my head hits the pillow. Other nights I turn in, but my mind refuses to turn off. My thoughts spin in circles thinking of all I've left undone and waiting for me the next day. But one day God showed me just how silly some of those circles are.

I am not, and never have been, a very athletic person. I think that I have "ball-phobia." If it's round and moves, I can't hit it or catch it. My husband, on the other hand, is Mr. Athlete. He played every sport in high school and even had a partial baseball scholarship to Clemson University.

My only athletic activity is snow skiing. For some reason, it just came naturally to me, probably because there is no ball involved. When Steve and I started dating,

I offered to teach him how to snow ski. He was aware of my athletic capabilities, or lack thereof, and decided that if I could do it, it would be a breeze for him.

We drove to Sugar Mountain, North Carolina for his first lesson. The key moves to learn when you first hit the slopes are how to slow down, how to stop, and how to get up once you fall. The rest is easy. The first thing Steve learned was how to get up, because the first thing he did was fall down.

To slow down, I taught Steve to turn his skis sideways and to weave back and forth across the mountain instead of going straight down. He would go straight for a while, and then when his speed picked up, he would turn his skis sideways to slow down. The only problem was, he had a tendency to turn them too far to the side and end up with the skis pointing up the mountain, which meant he would be going down the mountain backwards when he started moving again. This was not good!

Finally, he solved his problem. "When I try to turn, if I turn too much, I could just continue turning 360 degrees, making a complete circle," he explained to me. "That will still slow me down, and I won't end up going downhill backwards." It was a sight to behold, but it worked.

Near the end of the day, a lady who was very impressed with Steve's acrobatics, complimented him on his trick skiing. She raved, "Your circles are *beautiful!* Can you please teach me how to do them."

He obliged, of course, and performed a few circles for his admiring fan. She thought he was an expert skier and did not realize that he was just going in circles to survive.

Isn't that the way it is sometimes? We may look at others and think that they have it all together. We may want to be just like them—perform like them, be organized like them, or have well-behaved children like them. But the truth is, they are probably going in circles, just like we are, doing whatever it takes not to go downhill backwards.

But as children of God, we don't have to go in circles trying to keep up with the "spiritual Joneses." We simply need to rely on His power, rest in His strength, and keep our eyes on His Word. Wise King David once wrote, "Your Word is a lamp to my feet, and a light to my path" (Psalm 119:105). The good news is that the Lord's path is not circular or downhill; it's level and straight.

Be Still My Heart

I was lying in bed trying to fall asleep, but there was one small problem—my heart. It was beating too fast, and I couldn't get it to slow down.

In 1996 I noticed that my heart rate was a bit too fast, and that it was skipping beats like it had the hiccups. I was told that each little beat was important, and it's not good to leave any out. So I went to the doctor, and he discovered that I had Grave's disease, which is a hyperthyroid condition.

To find out more about the disease, I checked out a book from my local library with the creative title of *The Thyroid Book.* I had to laugh when I read the description of a person with hyperthyroidism. This could have been taken from a book titled, *Understanding Your Two-Year-Old,* or better yet, *Understanding the Mother of a Two-Year-Old.*

The following are some of the common symptoms of Grave's disease: muscle weakness, nervousness, irritability, short attention span, a decrease in ability to concentrate, a feeling of fatigue and exhaustion, a feeling of being "wired" or that your motor is always running, disturbed sleep pattern with frequent waking during the night, inability to achieve a relaxed state of restful sleep, great difficulty maintaining sufficient focus and concentration, jumpiness, and difficulty remaining in the same place for any length of time. The person with Grave's disease is always on the move. Even when sitting, movement of your arms and legs and changes of position in the chair may be frequent. Even though tired, the person with Grave's disease can "get so much more done."

Either the fellow who wrote the book was very smart or very confused. I had been like this since birth. As a matter-of-fact, most of the kids in the preschool nursery at my church fit this description! So I didn't think Grave's disease was any big deal.

Eventually, however, I did have to start taking an anti-thyroid medication to slow down my metabolism and my heart rate. The problem was, I liked being wired. (I like to think of it as being highly motivated.) I liked getting a lot done. So what if I couldn't sit still or concentrate, and was irritable, wired, and jumpy. So what if I couldn't achieve a relaxed state or stay in one place any length of time. I got a lot done, and wasn't that what being a wife and mother was all about?

But there was one small problem. It was a matter of the heart. My heart was getting tired, and I wasn't even forty yet. My little pump was being worked overtime, skipping beats and racing when it should have been resting. Heart rates over 110 are okay if you've just finished an Olympic race, but not if you're lying in bed trying to go to sleep. So I took my medication, and my heart said "thanks."

It's always a matter of the heart. So many things affect it: things we see, things we do, and things we love. The Bible has a lot to say about the heart, and it's not referring to the pump or the valentine, but rather the seat of mental and moral activity, the hidden springs of the personal life. It is where we are cleansed (Acts 15:9), troubled (John 14:1), grieved (Romans 4:2), feel joy (John 1622), and experience desires (John 5:28). The heart affects our perceptions (Matthew 9:4), understanding (Luke 13:15), conscience (Acts 2:32), intentions (Hebrews 4:12), will (Romans 6:17), and faith (Mark 11:28). Most importantly, the heart is where we ask our Savior to reside.

While there is so much good associated with the heart, there is also bad. Scripture says, "the heart is deceitful above all things" (Jeremiah 17:9 NIV). It just depends on who's in control—the Holy Spirit or the unholy flesh.

The thyroid gland is not bad in itself. But if it's out of balance, it can cause all kinds of problems, especially with the heart. Money is not bad in itself, but out of balance, it can wreak all kinds of havoc, especially on the spiritual heart. A myriad of good things, when they are out of balance in our lives, cause our spiritual hearts to dysfunction, and that affects the rest of the body of Christ.

So now I keep tabs on my heart. I may not get as much done as I used to, but that's okay. I also keep tabs on my spiritual heart and ask God to show me when my life is getting out of balance. When that happens, I take my *meditation,* rest in Him, and follow the Great Physician's orders.

Would You Be Afraid?

"Mommy, Mommy, I can't sleep. I'm afraid of the dark."

What parent hasn't heard those words at one time or another. While fear of the dark may not be robbing me of rest, fear of the future can. But God sent a little girl to teach me just how to look fear in the face and find peace and rest.

She was among an eager group of four-year-old children crowded around my feet as I taught their Sunday school lesson. They listened intently while I told them about Jesus and His disciples trapped in a thunderstorm on the Sea of Galilee.

"The winds *bleeeeeew* and rocked the little boat back and forth, back and forth. The waves were *soooooo* big, they splashed over the wooden sides and got the men all wet. Then water started to fill up the boat. And do you know what happens when a boat gets full of water?"

"It sinks," they chimed together.

"That's right." I continued with a concerned look on my face. "Also the lightning was *soooooo* bright, it looked like fire in the sky. And the thunder was *soooooo* loud, they could feel it vibrate in their chests." I didn't mention it, but I thought about how those men probably yearned for a place to rest. But none was available, or so it seemed.

After painting this picture of impending doom and thinking that I would have my pint-sized audience just a little worried about the fate of these men trapped in a storm, I asked the question, "Now if *you* were in a tiny boat, caught in a terrible storm like this, would *you* be afraid?"

One precious little girl, confident and unshaken by the entire scenario, shrugged her shoulders and replied, "Not if Jesus was in the boat with me."

I will never forget her answer. This is the key that calms all my worries and fears. Just as the storm raged all around the disciples, many times the storms of life rage around me: a friend discovers she has cancer, a husband loses his job, or a child is born with birth defects. These are storms with waves of emotions so high that our lifeboats fill with tears and appear that they could sink at any moment. Waves of fear rock our boats and threaten to spill us into the depths of despair without even lifejackets to keep us afloat.

"Tell me, would you be afraid?"

"Not if Jesus was in the boat with me."

He is. He said in His Word that He would never leave us nor forsake us (Deuteronomy 31:6,8; Joshua 1:5; Hebrews 13:5). Although our pain may be great, we don't need to be afraid that the storms of life will destroy us, because God is in the boat with us, and that should give us great rest and peace.

Collect Call

Beside my bed, cradled on the nightstand, sits my white, slim-line telephone. Now I realize this is probably a huge mistake. Those two objects are as diametrically opposed as crashing cymbals in a hushed library. My bed beckons me to relax, and the phone demands that I get busy. How strange that the Lord would use this rest-robbing, ringing machine to teach me how to rest in who I am in Him.

One warm Saturday in early September, I listened restlessly to a speaker at our church's annual ladies' retreat in Lake Lure, North Carolina. One of her topics of discussion included a segment on self-acceptance. She began, "What do you do or who do you look to for self-acceptance? Do you look to your friends for positive strokes? To your children's performance or behavior? To your husband's success?"

I was having trouble paying attention, so the Lord decided to teach me a little object lesson to drive home the speaker's point. At the break, I slipped out to use the camp's only pay phone to check in with my husband and son. I had not made a collect call in several years and was surprised at the computerization of the whole process. After I dialed the number, a prerecorded message answered my call rather than a human operator. The computerized operator asked, "What kind of call would you like to make: collect, person-to-person, or direct? Speak now." I answered, "Collect." Then the mechanical operator said, "At the sound of the tone, state your name." Feeling rather foolish in a roomful of women, I waited for the tone and said, "Sharon," into the receiver. Finally, after my nonconversation with the nonoperator, our home phone rang. Who should answer the call but another nonperson, my answering machine, with my voice!

So here I am, placing a collect call to myself, from myself, by myself! This is how it went: The computerized operator said, "Hello, you have a collect call from . . . (my voice said) 'Sharon.'" At the same time, my voice on the answering machine said, "Hello. You have reached the Jaynes' residence. We are unable to answer the phone at this time. At the sound of the beep, please leave a message, and we will return your call as soon as possible." In the middle of my nice little message on the answering machine, the mechanical operator asked, "Will you accept the charge?"

I just sat there for a moment. What did I expect to hear? The whole episode was absurd! So I did the only thing I could do. For the first time in my life, I hung up on myself! I turned to one of the other ladies in the room and said, "I guess I should have waited to see if I would have accepted my own collect call. Then I would know if I truly have self-acceptance." We all chuckled.

But as I walked outside, the Lord asked, "Well, do you?" I then realized what the speaker was trying to teach us that hot, muggy day. When I look to my own abilities to find self-worth and acceptance, it is just as fruitless as placing a collect call to myself and reaching my answering machine. When I look at my accomplishments, my children, my husband, and friends to find my value as a person, I will always come up short. I could have stayed on that phone forever and my voice on my answering machine would never have said, "Yes, I'll accept and pay for the call." Likewise, it is only by looking at Christ in me and resting in Him that I will ever find total acceptance. And the good news is that He has already accepted the charges!

Bushwhacker

After ten years of active membership in our home church, my husband and I felt the Lord leading us to change to a different church body. It was a terribly difficult decision, because it was much like changing families.

A prerequisite for membership at our new church was the completion of "The Pastor's Inquiry Class." For six weeks, prospective members were required to attend a class in which the pastor explained the basics of the faith and the doctrines of this particular denomination. I had been a Christian for more than twenty-five years and felt this would probably be a waste of time. Nevertheless, we went.

To my surprise, the time spent in this class was like a long, cool drink from a crystal-clear mountain stream. We did go over the basics: the sinfulness of man, the redeeming blood of Jesus Christ, and the promise of heaven for believers. We went back to our roots and were reminded once again of the Father's great love for us.

As I was thinking about how I had been blessed by attending the pastor's class, the Lord tapped me on the shoulder and said, "Remember the bushes? You've just had *your* bushes cut back."

We had been in our present home for ten years and had planted every bush and grass seed on our property. The bushes were finally looking beautifully mature and established when one day my husband said, "Honey, it's time to cut the bushes back."

"Cut the bushes back! What do you mean cut the bushes back?" I repeated. "You mean *trim* the bushes, don't you?"

"No," he stated matter-of-factly. "I mean cut them all the way back to the trunk. Cut all the leaves off with nothing left but a few bare limbs."

I was horrified when I realized he was not kidding. Evidently, the bushes looked great on the outside, having finally reached maturity, but the problem was that in the center of each bush, underneath all the

pretty, new, green growth, there were no leaves. Inside, the bush appeared dead.

Steve went outside and cut the bushes almost to the ground, leaving nothing but pitiful, stubby nubs. I was so angry! I just knew he had killed them and doubted his reassurance that they would come back prettier than before. I told him, "You better pray those bushes will come back, or you'll be in a serious doghouse!"

Much to my surprise and Steve's relief, the bushes quickly sprouted new growth. Because the roots were well established, they grew back more beautiful than ever, with green on the *inside* as well as the outside. They were rejuvenated!

That's what happened to me in the pastor's class. We "cut back the bushes." My "bushes" were never dead on the inside; it was just that I needed to trim back the excess so the Light could promote new growth. Pastor Reeder cut back the bushes by returning to the basics—the root—the beginnings of our faith. It was wonderful to have the Light shining on my bare, inner self again.

Dr. Snow White and the Seven Dwarfs

After a week of traveling, there's nothing quite like the feeling of crawling into your own bed and burying your head in your own pillow. Sometimes it's just good to know that some things never change. My husband is one of those constants in my life.

Steve became a Christian in high school and has never wavered from his strong faith. He was never a rebellious sort as a child—just a good old, all-American kid. As an adult, he has been a model citizen and exemplary Christian. I guess you could say he is the male version of Snow White.

One problem Steve does have is understanding the mysteries of women. To top it off, the poor fellow is a dentist with seven female employees (translation: seven sets of hormones and seven sets of PMS). They are all wonderful Christians, but women nonetheless.

As I listened to his stories about them and sensed his frustration in trying to figure them out, I kept getting this picture in my mind of "Dr. Snow White and the Seven Dwarfs." If you remember, the dwarfs' names in the original story were Doc, Bashful, Happy, Sleepy, Sneezy, Dopey, and Grumpy. I decided what he needed to do was to make nametags of the seven dwarfs and put them in a basket. Each morning, when the women came in the office, they could reach into the basket and pull out a nametag that expressed how they were feeling on that particular day. It would take the guesswork out of it, and Steve would know how to respond to each woman on any given day.

Of course, at the end of each day, he would have to collect the nametags, put them back into the basket, and bring them home so I could pick out which dwarf I was on that day. Poor men! We women do make it hard on them.

But thank goodness, God never changes. The Bible is full of different names for God that describe the unchangeable characteristics of His nature. He is Jehovah-jireh, the Lord that provides; Jehovah-rapha, the Lord that heals; Jehovah-shalom, the Lord our peace; Jehovah-shammah, the Lord who is there. What a comfort to know that we don't have to depend on a God who is always changing like we are! Instead, our Lord "is the same yesterday and today and forever" (Hebrews 13:8 NIV). And in that we can rest.

Lame Man Dancing

"I'll never rest until I get this right!"

How many times I have uttered those words. Then one summer, the Lord taught me just what "getting it right" truly meant.

My husband and I escaped to the captivating island of Bermuda where the water is crystal clear and the bluest of blues, and the air is filled with the scent of blooming hibiscus. Our vacation was complete with long romantic walks on white sandy beaches, splashing waves on limestone rock jetties, and discoveries of secluded ocean-carved caves.

On one particular evening, Steve and I went on a dining adventure to a five-star restaurant filled with men and women dressed in their finest evening apparel. The semicircular dining room was lined with glass overlooking the Atlantic Ocean and framed the flaming orange-red of the setting sun.

In one corner of the dining area, a four-man orchestra filled the room with fluid sounds of music from the forties and fifties. At one point, Steve urged, "Come on, Sharon. Let's take a spin on the dance floor."

"No way," I replied, "Nobody else is out there. I'm not going to be the only one on the floor with everyone staring at me. Suppose we mess up? I'd be embarrassed. It's been a long time since we've danced, and I don't remember all the steps. Let's wait until there are some other people dancing. Then I'll go."

Finally, the first couple approached the floor. They looked like professional dancers, moving as one and never missing a beat. This did not encourage me at all but only strengthened my resolve. Then couple number one was joined by couple number two, whose steps weren't quite as perfect.

"Okay, now I'll go," I agreed. "But let's head for the back corner where nobody can see us."

So off we went to our little spot on the wooden dance floor and tried to remember how to fox trot. As we were moving as two, I noticed a fourth couple approach the floor. They came with confidence—no hesitation, no timidity. Only the man of this pair sat in a wheelchair.

He was a slightly balding, large-framed man with a neatly trimmed beard. On his left hand, he wore a white glove, perhaps to cover some skin disease or disfigurement. Both were dressed in evening wear, but the most beautiful part of their dress was the radiant smiles they both wore. Their love for each other lit up the room.

As the band played a peppy beat, the wife held her love's healthy right hand and danced with him. He never rose from the wheelchair that had become his legs, but they didn't seem to care. They came together and separated like expert dancers. He spun her around as she stooped to conform to her husband's seated position. Lovingly, like a little fairy child, she danced around his chair while his laughter became the fifth instrument in the small orchestra. Even though his feet did not move from their metal resting places, his shoulders swayed in perfect time and his eyes danced with hers.

My heart was so moved by their obvious love that I had to turn my head and bury my face on Steve's shoulder so no one would see the tears streaming down my cheeks. As I did, I saw every person in this rigid, formal dining room with tears trickling down their cheeks. All around the room, linen napkins dabbed tearful eyes. This portrait of love and devotion even transfixed the band.

Then the music slowed to a lazy romantic melody. The wife pulled a chair up beside her husband, but facing in the opposite direction, and they held one another in a dancer's embrace. One arm was extended as the other was placed on her love's shoulder. Cheek to cheek, they swayed to the piano's love song. At one point, they both closed their eyes, and I imagined they dreamed of an earlier time when they were not restrained by his chair.

After watching this incredible display of love and courage, I realized that my inhibitions of not wanting others to watch me because of my imperfect steps were gone. The Lord spoke to my heart in a powerful way:

Sharon, I want you to notice, who moved this crowd to tears? Was it couple number one, with their perfect steps? Or was it the last couple who not only did not have perfect steps, but had no steps at all? No, my child, it was the display of love—not perfection—that had an effect on the people watching.

My steps on a dance floor, or more importantly in life, will never be perfect. So many times, I am afraid to step out into the spotlight, even though God may be calling my name. Or when the Lord calls me to walk down a certain path, I sometimes catch myself arguing, "Well, Lord, there's no one else on that path. If I'm the only one out there, people might be watching. Suppose I mess up? They'll notice. They might even laugh. I think I'll just wait until someone else goes out there first. Then I'll go. Check back with me in a few months . . . or a few years."

But the Lord doesn't expect my steps to be perfect. He just expects me to be obedient, to take the first step, and to let Him do the rest. The man in the wheelchair never moved his feet; his wife moved for him. I need to remember that the Lord will do that for me. I also need to remember that the world is not desperately looking for perfect steps. The masses aren't impressed by perfect people who live in perfect houses with perfect children. They are impressed by love: genuine God-inspired love. That's what moves a crowd.

That night, by the beautiful shores of Bermuda, God sent a lame man to teach me how to dance.

Dear Lord,

Thank You for making this lamb lie down in green pastures when my tendency is to continue walking until my shaky little legs collapse. A sheep was never intended to be used as a pack animal, yet I strap burdens on my back that make me weak, weary, and worn-out.

Forgive me when I foolishly jump in and try to take control of every situation. Help me remember that it is only when I keep my eyes fixed on Your face and follow in Your steps that I will stay on the right path.

Thank You for leading me, stilling my heart, and never changing. Thank You that I don't have to worry about how to accomplish all that You've called me to do, because I know that You will do it for me; all I have to do is obey Your still small voice. In You, I am refreshed, restored, and renewed.

Amen.

The Bathroom

Clean at Last

The business of living can become rather grueling at times, leaving us grimy, sticky, sweaty, soiled, and tarnished. Grocery-store shelves are bulging with a smorgasbord of products to cleanse our bodies from head to toe. We soak, scrub, sluff, brush, bathe, buff, purify, clarify, deodorize, sanitize, lather, rinse, and repeat.

When I was a child, I was taught, "Cleanliness is next to godliness." Now that I am an adult, I've learned that cleanliness *is* godliness. No, I'm not talking about the freshness that results from a bar of soap or a fragrant bottle of bath beads. I'm talking about the purity of heart that comes from knowing Jesus Christ and being washed by the Word of God. But no matter what brand of soap we use to scrub the outside, there's no man-made product available to cleanse the part that really matters—the inside.

Step into the sauna of God's love and let the Scriptures pour over your soul. You'll emerge wearing the fragrance of Christ and feeling clean at last.

The Auctioning Block

When I was in my late teens, I had an unusual fetish for old, beat-up, antique furniture. While most of my friends were at the malls shopping for clothes, I was at estate sales, flea markets, yard sales, and auctions hunting for antiques. Often when I brought my purchases home, my family would roll their eyes in disgust and say, "I can't believe you paid money for that dirty piece of junk." But I never saw my purchases as junk. They just needed a little work—okay, a lot of work!

At one estate sale, I spied a little drop-leaf kitchen table with three spindle-back chairs. I could just imagine a sweet little old lady spending many years sitting at that very table drinking her morning coffee. The set was painted hospital green, but it had great potential. Obviously, the other bidders didn't appreciate its fine qualities, because ten minutes and thirty-five dollars later, the set was mine. I was sure I had saved the table and chairs from becoming kindling for someone's fire. I brought the dinette set home, all excited about my great buy, but I couldn't understand why no one else shared my enthusiasm.

"Sharon, do you realize how much time and energy it is going to take to make that old green rickety table look even slightly presentable?" they asked. At that point in my life, I had a lot more time than money, so the time wasn't a problem.

Refinishing furniture is a dirty, grueling task, and refinishing this table and chairs was no exception. First I stripped off the paint with paint remover, which not only removes paint but eats through latex gloves and layers of skin. I discovered that not only had the table been green, it had also been blue, and before that white. But underneath it all was pure walnut!

The paint remover raised the grain of the wood, so I had to go back and sand it smooth. If the sanding isn't done well, the finished product will always be a little rough. A few joints had come loose from wear and tear, and I had to glue them back together. Then I applied a warm walnut stain that deepened its color and made the beautiful pattern of the wood grain stand out. Finally, I applied polyurethane to seal and protect the piece.

As I worked, I began to think of the old broken table as a symbol of my own life. I was also on the auction block, and God paid a price for me with His Son's precious blood. I was saved from someone's fire. I had layers and layers of old self that hid the beauty of God's creation. These layers had to be stripped off by crucifying my flesh with its passions and desires. This raised my grain, but God sanded me with life experiences and trials. God glued my loose joints and mended my broken pieces, for He heals the brokenhearted and binds up their wounds. God put a sealer not only on me but also in me—the Holy Spirit—who is given to me as a seal and a promise.

I sat in the garage looking at my finished work and thinking about all that God had done for me. My mom opened the door, looked at the old table, and said, "I never thought something so ugly could turn out so beautiful."

"Amen," I said.

More than twenty-five years later, that little table and chairs still sits in my family room as a reminder of what God has done in my life. As they say in the fashion world, "it's really me."

Three Squirrels

It's a common scene. A rambunctious five-year-old boy emerges from the bathroom and holds out his hands for inspection. Then his mother turns him around and points him back to the sink to scrub some more. Sometimes it's just hard to get everything clean all at the same time, whether it's a little boy's hands or a grown woman's heart.

Even messier than small boys are pesky squirrels. They can be a real challenge. I love birds. I love bird feeders. But I detest squirrels. I can fill a bird feeder one day, and a squirrel, hanging upside down by one grubby paw while waving at me with its other paw, can empty it the next and scatter seed all over the ground.

We've tried all kinds of contraptions to keep the squirrels off of the bird feeders. They seem to help for a few days, but in the end, the squirrels always figure out a way to overcome the obstacle. They find a way to get over it, under it, around it, or even sit on it.

One summer, I noticed that there always seemed to be three squirrels at my bird feeder but never more than three. A neighbor of mine had a squirrel cage in which you could catch the little "darlings" and take them to a better place (which was any place other then my yard)! I decided to give the squirrel cage a try.

I shared the idea with my skeptical husband and explained, "All I have to do is put some food—birdseed, of course—in the cage and leave the door open. When the squirrel creeps into the cage, the door closes and traps the fellow inside. It will not hurt him at all. Then I can take him out into the country where he can, as Spock says, 'live long and prosper.' It will be easy."

Steve said, "I'll remember those words in a few weeks, especially the last one—easy."

I was getting a little excited about winning this war with the squirrels. Victory was in the air!

The first day met with great success. Thirty minutes after the bait was set, I had a conquest. As I approached the caged animal, I wasn't sure who was more afraid: the squirrel or me. I had actually not been up close and personal with a squirrel before, and from the squirrel's reaction to me, he had never been up close and personal with a human before. I donned my thick gloves, lifted the cage, and took my furry friend to his new home out in the country. When I opened the cage door to let him out, he never looked back, but shot out of the cage like a speeding bullet. At the end of the day, I had made three trips to the country, leaving behind all three of the squirrels. That night, sleep was sweet.

You can imagine my horror when I arose the next morning to look out at the bird feeder and see squirrels—three squirrels. Were these the same squirrels? I felt like I was in a rerun of *Homeward Bound,* with squirrels playing the parts of the two dogs and a cat. A call to the veterinarian assured me that the squirrels on day two were not the same squirrels from day one. He said that as long as they had water and food where they were, they would just stay put. So I repeated the previous day's journeys to the country with three new little friends.

On the third morning of the battle, I was almost afraid to look. Peeping out from behind the curtain, what did I see? You guessed it, three squirrels at the feeder. This was ridiculous. Why three? Did they have some kind of honor code that said, "only three to a feeder at one time?" How did those three know that the other two sets of three were gone?

I set the trap, caught the squirrels, and then delivered the squirrels to the country. I was not happy. Day four . . . same story. Three squirrels. Three trips to the country. Only this time, I drove directly back to my neighbor's house to return the squirrel cage. They weren't surprised by my disgust; their experience had been similar. For every squirrel they took to the country, another one had shown up in their yard. The squirrels still amaze me. There were always three little pests—no more, no less. When I got rid of three, three more moved in.

There are attitudes, behaviors, and thoughts in my life that I've tried just as determinedly to eliminate. It seems that just as soon as victory is in sight in one area, the Lord shows me another one where I need to apply a scrub brush. The good news is that He wants to do the scrubbing for me! I simply have to sit still and let Him do His work, cleaning up one area at a time.

I still have the bird feeder. I still have the squirrels. Three squirrels as a matter of fact, and I still have some internal pests God is working on.

Beached

Have you ever gone to the powder room after a lovely dinner with friends, but instead of a shiny nose, you discover the remains of the entree on your chin! How embarrassing! But I guess that's what mirrors are for. The Holy Spirit is a mirror that points out our blemishes and dirty spots. But the difference is, we don't have to be in the powder room to see them. We can be in the grocery story, on the playground, or even at the beach.

I've always loved the beach. My favorite pastime is to pitch my umbrella as the sun rises over the ocean's horizon, hunker down with a good book and thermos of iced tea, and return to the cottage when the evening sky grows too dark to read the words on my page.

Besides enjoying God's creation, I also enjoy watching His creatures. You can learn a lot about human nature by watching people at the beach. Teenage girls position themselves strategically to be noticed by muscle-bound young men strutting down the sandy runway. Dads pass footballs to admiring sons, who are delighted to spend some time with their heroes. Moms in skirted swimsuits look at bikini-clad teens in disgust, while secretly lamenting bygone days of flat tummies and slender thighs. Little tots squeal in delight at the sudden freedom to play in the sand with no one telling them to stay out of the dirt. Their tiny feet are in constant motion like little windup toys running from Mom to the water and back to Mom again. Have you ever noticed that no child under the age of four walks at the beach? It's a gallop, a skip, or a sprint. But it's never a walk.

One beautiful summer day, I was casually reclining in my lounge chair, not reading, but people watching. I noticed an Asian family on my immediate right. The small-framed mother was kneeling by her adult son and wiping the sand off of his feet with a towel. Then she humbly slipped his shoes on his clean feet. The young man casually read a book, never looking up as his subservient mother waited on him—literally, hand and foot.

How disgusting, I thought to myself. *This is America. Let the boy wipe his own feet.* I believe in being submissive, but this was taking it a bit too far. I made a mental note to have a talk with this woman. With that thought, I closed my eyes and took a little snooze while the sea breeze gave me a gentle backrub.

That evening, after showering and removing all traces of salt and sand, my husband, son, and I headed for the elevator to search out a restaurant for dinner. Who should be sharing the ride down with us but the family with the feet-wiping mother? We reached the ground floor, and the men parted to let the mother pass. Then her son awkwardly followed behind. His legs were fitted with metal braces, and his arms were cuffed with metal crutches that swung forward and propelled his lower body toward the door.

The elevator emptied, and the mirrored walls seemed to reflect my judgmental attitude. I was so ashamed; I wanted to stay and ride back up to my room. Subservient indeed! Now a whole new list of words describing this mother flooded my mind: loving, tender, caring, pained, sacrificial, and brave.

"Lord," I prayed, "Forgive me for jumping to conclusions and making quick judgments. Forgive my critical spirit. Bless that mother and her child. Give him strength of body and her strength of heart."

You can learn a lot about human nature by watching people on the beach. That day, I learned a lot about my own and about how dependent I am on my Father to cleanse my unruly thoughts.

City Slickers

When Steven was a preschool bucking bronco, I had to rope him in before corralling him into the bathtub. In somewhat similar fashion, God sometimes has to lasso my galloping thoughts as well. At a rodeo one night, I got to see just how that's done.

There we sat—three city slickers among whoopin,' hollerin' locals at the Saturday night rodeo in Jackson Hole, Wyoming. It wasn't hard to tell the tourists from the locals. There were Reeboks among cowboy boots, scarves among bandannas, chewing gum among chewing tobacco, baseball caps among ten-gallon, wide-brim hats, and warm fringed suede jackets among skimpy nylon Windbreakers. (Who knew that temperatures on a July night would plummet to thirty-five degrees when the sun set behind the Grand Teton Range?)

The cowboys' skills entertained and amazed those of us who thought a bronco was a four-wheel drive vehicle. Cowboys, young and old, rode bucking broncos, raced around barrels, and conquered angry bulls. But the most thrilling event was the lassoing contest.

The announcer introduced, "And now here's the Jackson Hole High School lassoing champion for 1997."

My son looked at me in amazement. "They have lassoing as a school sport? They do this in P.E.? Well, I guess they don't have a golf team."

We all sat on the edge of our seats as the cowboy waited, poised in his saddle, anticipating the calf's release from the chute. The corral door swung open, and the calf burst out of the gate. The cowboy, with lasso hand, raced after the bucking, twisting, galloping animal; lassoed its neck; threw it to the ground; quickly wrapped the rope around its legs; tied them securely in place, and immediately jumped up and raised his arms in victory. As the victor stood receiving his applause, his trained steed took three steps back to secure the rope in place. "Yep, that little heifer ain't goin' nowhere," the horse seemed to say.

The timer continued to run for a few seconds to make sure the calf was indeed captive. Then the cowboy's time was posted on the scoreboard. Time and time again, cowhands lassoed little calves, secured their captives, and raised their hands in victory. Only a few times did a calf escape the rope and make its way out the door on the other end.

I'll admit that I was feeling a bit sorry for the little calves, even though they were released as soon as the time was logged. But the Lord prodded my mind and told me to look and learn. This event was a perfect picture of what Paul described in 2 Corinthians 10:5 when he said, "We are destroying speculation and every lofty thing raised up against the knowledge of God, and we are taking every thought captive to the obedience of Christ."

Those calves reminded me of wild and woolly thoughts that burst forth from the stable of my mind at times: negative, rebellious, fearful, angry, worrisome, jealous, thoughts that are untamed and unruly, bucking, jumping, and running wild across pleasant plains. And my reaction should be that of the cowboy: ride up hot on the thought's heels, lasso it, tie it up, and throw it in the dust. My response should be just like the cowboy's trusty, trained horse that automatically, because of practice, takes three steps backward to make sure the negative thought "ain't goin' nowhere."

The picture was branded in my memory. Trained because of practice. Taking every thought captive. Yes siree. Let's lasso those thoughts, little sister, tie 'em up, and throw 'em back in the dust where they came from in the first place.

Making sure our thoughts are clean may take a lot of effort and practice, but in the end, we can join the rodeo cowboy and raise our arms in victory and listen for the applause of heaven.

God's Speedometer

Clean is a relative term. A teenager's definition of a clean room and his mother's may be miles apart. The nurse who prepares a sterile operating room and the custodian who dusts the waiting room have totally different goals in mind. God's idea of a clean life is in sharp contrast to our's. Somewhere along the way, we have to decide whose standard we are going to follow.

I met my husband in a Bible study group in college and quickly learned that he was a frugal, industrious, and resourceful young man. On our first date, he came to pick me up in his ten-year-old Volkswagen Beetle that he had purchased for seven hundred and twenty-five dollars. He says it was yellow. I say it was beige. Regardless of the color, this fine piece of machinery had several remarkable features.

I don't know if it was the weather or our excitement on our first date, but as soon as we got into the car, the windows fogged up. As we drove down Franklin Street in Chapel Hill, he asked, "Sharon, will you please get the defroster from the glove compartment and help me out so I can see?" I reached in the compartment to pull out the defroster—a small towel. Of course, I was impressed with his great wit and was delighted to ride around campus, wiping the front windshield as we went along. Isn't it amazing the perspective we have of inconveniences when love is new?

Another amazing feature of this "beige" car was its ability to plow through the snow like a miniature snowmobile. In the South, it's a big deal when we get more than a few flakes, because we're not prepared for big snows. So during our first spring break when it snowed eighteen inches, the town was paralyzed. Everyone was either homebound or sliding off the road or into one another on slick city streets. Everyone, that is, except Steve and his little "Punch Bug." He puttered around town like *The Little Engine that Could* and was the envy of all the other shiny new cars on campus.

But perhaps the most remarkable feature of his VW was the speedometer. It didn't work. The speedometer broke when the odometer hit two hundred thousand miles and never left zero again.

"Steve," I asked, "If your speedometer doesn't work, how do you know how fast you're going?"

"Well," he answered, "I just pay attention to how fast cars around me are traveling and pace myself according to their speed. Besides, I can tell when to change gears and about how fast I'm going by how much the car shakes!" So Steve traveled around town and on highways, with no earthly idea of his exact speed.

We were married ten months after our first date, between the last session of summer school and the fall semester. It was about ninety-eight degrees on the August day Steve drove from Charlotte to Rocky Mount, North Carolina for our wedding weekend. His VW had no air-conditioning (of course), so he left Charlotte in the wee hours on a Friday morning to avoid the midday heat. Because it was so early, there was virtually no traffic. Now that may seem like a dream come true for most people, but Steve *needed* traffic. His points of reference were missing, and he couldn't judge his speed.

About two hours into the trip, Steve saw a blue light flashing in his rearview mirror, and his heart sank as he realized he was being pulled over by a state patrolman.

"Where you going in such a hurry, young man?" the officer asked.

"Actually, sir, I'm on my way to get married."

The patrolman just smiled as he handed Steve the ticket and said, "Well, don't let this ruin your day."

Your day! Steve thought. *What about ruin your insurance and your budget—the budget of a guy working his way through school who had to have a yard sale to go on a honeymoon!*

Well, he didn't let it ruin his day. It was one of the most beautiful days of our lives. But I was really angry with that patrolman. The truth is, cars are not intended to be driven without a speedometer, and folks, neither are we. *Our* speedometer is the Word of God. It's a wonderful love letter written to teach us how to drive safely through life. We aren't supposed to judge our speed or lifestyle on the basis of what's going on around us. We are to use His Word as our guide.

Romans 12:2 says, "Do not be conformed to this world, but be transformed by the renewing of your mind." Yet sometimes I tend to gauge my performance by what other people are doing. And those who don't know the Word of God have no other choice *but* to judge their lives by the lives of others.

However, when we use the world's speedometer instead of God's Word, chances are the Patrolman (the Holy Spirit) is going to pull us over and write a ticket. We shouldn't be surprised when we see that big blue light in our rearview mirror.

The good news is, no matter how many times the Holy Spirit has to pull us over, no matter how many times we fail, no matter how messy we appear to be, the wedding is still going to take place. The Scripture says we are the bride of Christ. One day, He will come to take us to the home that He has prepared for us, and there's nothing that will stand in His way.

Into the Hands of Man

When our children are little tots and too young to bathe themselves, we parents have to do it for them. Likewise, we have to clean them up on their insides a little. I was reminded of that when studying the story of how God cleaned up King David's act.

During my quiet time, I had been studying 2 Samuel and the ups and downs of King David. In the last chapter, David decided to take a census. This was a bad idea. Even his friend, Joab, tried to talk him out of it, but David numbered Israel anyway.

The problem was, the Lord had not instructed David to do this. It was not war time or tax time. David just momentarily had a pride problem and was placing his trust in numbers instead of God.

Nine months later, the head count tallied a 130,000 valiant soldiers. When the census was complete, David felt a little guilty about his actions and realized that he had acted foolishly. (It makes me wonder what he was thinking during those nine long months.)

God was really angry with David, but He forgave him. Even though David was forgiven, he still had to be disciplined and face the consequences of his actions. As my husband would say, "He still had to take his licks." The Lord gave David his choice of three punishments, none of which was very appealing: famine for seven years, pursuit by enemies for three years, or pestilence by God for three days. David chose the latter, his reason being, "I am in great distress. Let us now fall into the hand of the LORD for His mercies are great, but do not let me fall into the hands of man" (2 Samuel 24:14).

This story took me back a few years when my son, Steven, was faced with a similar decision. Steven had told a lie. I don't remember what the lie was, but lying just doesn't fly at our house. I forgave him, but he still had to be disciplined. I told him, "Son, you have a choice. No TV or Nintendo for a week, or five licks with a paddle now."

He thought about this for a few seconds and then asked, "Who'll be giving the 'licks,' you or Daddy?"

I was shocked! "Does it matter?" I questioned.

He replied, "You bet it matters."

My husband just laughed and said, "I guess all 'licks' are not created equal." Apparently, mine were a little less effective. Like David, Steven chose the route that would seemingly be over the quickest. Unlike David, he *did* "fall into the hand of man,"—the man of the house that is!

A Way of Escape

Keeping the dirt and grime of life from collecting on our hands, feet, and minds is an overwhelming task at times. Temptations are at every turn: an unkind word, a deviation from the straight path, or ideas that are contrary to Scripture. But I take great comfort in knowing that God always has an escape route in place. The question is, "Will I take it?"

A little fluorescent-green fly with transparent wings positioned itself on the dashboard of my car, like a runner on its mark waiting for the shot to be fired. Then it torpedoed into the windshield at breakneck speed, only to bounce back like it had been hit by an electrical current. Confused by this invisible barrier, it perched on the dashboard once again and strategized its next move, while rubbing its tiny little hands together.

Suddenly, it shot forward with all its might, only to once again bounce off the force field and land panting on the dash. Then in one final act of desperation and frustration, it angrily attacked the glass at seven pops per second.

Feeling rather sorry for this insect, I rolled down my window and spoke softly to my captured friend. "Look, little fly, the window is open. Feel the wind. Here it is—your way of escape."

But the fly was knocked silly and lay recuperating on the dashboard, oblivious to the freedom just inches away. After a few seconds, I realized that it was not going to escape on its own volition, so I used my hand to shoo it in the direction of the open window. It resisted like a young puppy on a leash but finally made its way to the opening. However, instead of jumping at the chance of freedom, the little green fly with the bulging eyes just sat there with its wings pinned back by the sixty-mile-per-hour winds.

"Go on," I coaxed. "What are you afraid of?" I could not believe that I was talking to a fly and taking my eyes off the road to rescue a bug. Finally it became evident that Mr. Fly was not going to take this leap of faith, so I gave it that little extra push it needed, and off it flew.

Why was I so concerned for this silly fly? Pity, I guess. It was trying so hard to get free, and yet the way of escape was so close. This is a common problem for flies and mortal men alike. In 1 Corinthians 10:13, it says, "No temptation has overtaken you but such as is common to man; and God is faithful, who will not allow you to be tempted beyond what you are able, but with the temptation will provide the way of escape also, that you may be able to endure it." Whether it's King David being tempted to glance at Bathsheba taking a late-night bath on her rooftop or one of us being tempted to watch an unhealthy television program, there is always a way of escape. There is always an open window just a few steps away.

If we could hear the fly tell of its adventure of entrapment and escape, it might sound something like this: "I flew into a place where I thought I would find pleasure, but instead, I found bondage. When I tried to get away, some invisible force kept me a prisoner. I banged my head against an unseen barrier time and time again. As I staggered to gain my composure and wait for the room to stop spinning, I saw an open window and a big hand coaxing me to come. My faltering steps led me to a ledge where I felt the wind on my face. I stood on the edge of freedom unable to take that next step when that gentle hand gave me the push I needed, and out I flew. I was free."

A common tale of flies and men. Let's keep our eyes open to the way of escape and make a clean break from the temptations of each day.

Disclosing Tablets

Not many people consider brushing their teeth a spiritual experience. But when I worked as a dental hygienist, I saw lessons in several aspects of dentistry that applied to my walk with the God. For example, the Lord taught me a lesson with disclosing tablets to make me appreciate the cleansing power that He offered me at the cross.

Disclosing tablets are little red pills that patients chew to reveal how well they have brushed their teeth. If any plaque was missed during brushing, the disclosing tablet turns it bright red. The kids think of it as a lie-detector test.

One day, I thought about how glad I was that we don't have spiritual disclosing tablets. Can you imagine walking into church every Sunday and the pastor handing you a spiritual disclosing tablet? We would chew it up, and all of our failures and faults from the past week would show up bright red!

Just as I was having this horrible thought, another thought popped into my mind. We did have spiritual disclosing tablets. They weren't red and candy-like but were made of stone. There were two of them, with five laws written on each one. When people said their lives were clean, God used these disclosing tablets to show them where they had missed the mark.

I am so glad that we don't have to pass the spiritual disclosing-tablet test to get into the kingdom of God. As the doctors say, "studies have shown" that no one could pass. Jesus took the test for us, and because of Him, we can say, *Clean at last!*

Under Construction

When it comes to cleaning up my act, I've decided that I need more than a dainty little sign that reads, "Please do not disturb," hanging on my bathroom door. Instead, I need an orange-and-white construction barrel to barricade the area, with a posted warning sign that reads, "Slow—God at Work."

In North Carolina, our state bird is the cardinal and the state flower is the dogwood. I have decided that our state shrub should be the orange-and-white construction barrel.

Our town of two hundred thousand had a growth spurt that took us to five hundred thousand in the twinkling of an eye. Like that adolescent boy who suddenly has pants that are too short and ears that are too big, our town had schools that were too small and roads that were too narrow.

My family lived on the outskirts of town to avoid the hubbub of the inner city. But before long, the outskirts became the "in-skirts," and our quiet neighborhood, with a spine and six cul-de-sacs branching off to the left and right, became surrounded by major arteries, pumping cars around our quiet suburb.

My son's school was just five minutes from our home—at 10 A.M. that is. At 7:30 in the morning, the main road to the school became the road most traveled, and our trek became a thirty to thirty-five minute Oregon Trail experience. Our little two-lane road was definitely overworked and under paved!

During Steven's second-grade year, city workers lined the road with orange-and-white-striped, cone-shaped construction barrels. It was then that we knew this street was about to have triple-bypass surgery. I didn't know if I should be happy or sad. I knew construction would mean a smoother ride in the future but a slower commute in the present.

Bulldozers dug up one side of the road and turned the two lanes into one. Now we're talking congestive heart failure—mine! I tried to keep a good attitude about the bumpy road ahead, but after a few months, my attitude took a turn for the worse.

"I can't stand this dust!" I complained. "I can't stand this mud!" Steven didn't help with questions like, "Mommy, why does it take so many men to hold the flag?" or "Mommy, why are those ten men lying over in the grass and only two are working?" When my car started shaking and I took it in to see what the problem was, I nearly lost it when the repairman told me, "Mrs. Jaynes, there's nothing wrong with your car. You just have four bent rims from running over potholes." Orange is such an ugly color!

Then one day, two and a half years after the emergence of the despised orange barrels and construction signs (it gave new meaning to "slow men working"), a wonderful young man in a beautiful white truck, drove by, and one by one, he lifted the eyesores onto his flat bed and hauled the stacks of plastic away. Did I say *away?* Actually, he picked up the ugly things, turned the corner, and put them down another one of the main arteries that we traveled every day. This signaled that we were in for two more years of dust, broken pavement, and flagmen. *Warning! Road Construction Ahead!* Maybe "Bring Out the Barrels; We'll Have a Barrel of Fun" should be our state song.

No one likes road construction, except maybe flagmen, barrel manufacturers, and asphalt companies. Likewise, I certainly don't get excited when God comes by and plops an orange-and-white barrel down on some aspect of my life that needs overhauling. Unfortunately, I am definitely still under construction. I would love to live on "easy street," but more often than not, bulldozers are digging up one of my lanes and causing upheaval in my life. I have potholes and cracked pavement that need repairing, and instead of easy street, it's usually a road of hard knocks. I like the finished product, but I detest the work in progress.

Bill Gaither wrote a children's song that says, "He's still working on me, to make me what I ought to be. He may have had a day to make the moon and the stars, the sun and the earth and Jupiter and Mars. How lovely and patient He must be, 'cause He's still working on me."

Now when I see those orange barrels, I thank the Lord for His continuous construction work on my life. But I look forward to the day when I walk through the pearly gates of heaven and see the streets all clean and glistening, paved not with the asphalt of my humanity, but with the gold of Christ's glory. And there'll be no more construction barrels in sight!

Dear Lord,

I tried so hard to aim at being good, but my arrow kept missing the mark. I tried so hard to walk the straight and narrow, but I kept tripping over the shoestrings of my humanity. I tried so hard to say only words that were pure and pleasing, but corruption kept popping out of my mouth like a jack-in-the-box.

Thank You for the words in Romans 5:8, "But God demonstrates His own love toward us, in that while we were yet sinners, Christ died for us."

Thank You for the cleansing blood of Jesus Christ that did for me what I was not able to do for myself. Just as You cleansed Moses' leprous hand at the burning bush, so You have cleansed my leprous spirit. Now when I gaze intently into Your wonderful face and see my reflection in the twinkle of Your eye, I see a daughter of the King clothed in the righteousness of Christ's final obedience. And I can breathe a sigh of relief that says, Clean at last!

Amen.

The Hallway

Moving On

Of all the areas in a house, perhaps the hallway is the least celebrated. For centuries, it has been snubbed, slighted, and overlooked, and yet it's the artery through which the activities of daily life flow.

The hallway is more than just a corridor to take us from one room to another. It represents movement, progress, and growth. My well-worn carpet has felt the pitter-patter of little feet metamorphose into the heavy footsteps of a man's size-ten tennis shoe. Where once I had to stoop down to wash a toddler's precious fingerprints from its cream-colored walls; now I have to reach up to scrub teen-sized smudges.

Yes, it's more than two narrow walls and a thin strip of carpet. It's a place of passage, reminding me that in Christ, we are continually growing, maturing, and moving on.

Guess Who I Bumped into Today?

Perhaps the biggest roadblock that keeps us from moving forward and becoming all that God intends and accomplishing all that He desires, is fear. However, it is in facing our fears that we build our faith.

I know this is the twenty-first century, but I still get a little embarrassed shopping in the lingerie department. I realize that everybody wears underwear, but something about milling around racks of panties makes me uncomfortable.

One day while I was shopping, I noticed an elderly gentleman who looked even more uncomfortable than I did. Apparently, this man's wife was looking for some new bloomers, and he was trying his best to casually avoid the area altogether. The lingerie department was across the aisle from the children's clothing department. This elderly gentleman strolled up and down this buffer zone, taking an intense interest in the latest fall fashions for girls' sizes two to six-x. His head stayed sharply turned to the right to avoid peeping at the ladies' personal apparel on the left.

Mr. Man did a good job of not looking at the ladies unmentionables but a pretty bad job of looking where his steps were taking him. What he did not see was that he was on a direct collision course with a mannequin, scantily dressed in a transparent nightie. As he innocently strolled down toward the nightgowns on his left and the girls' plaid jumpers on his right, Mr. Man ran smack-dab into Ms. Mannequin, knocking her off of her stand. He spun around at breakneck speed, and with the agility of Superman, he caught Ms. Mannequin, nightie and all, just before she hit the floor. Before he could be caught red-handed (and red-faced), he placed Ms. Mannequin back on her stand, and as any gallant Southern gentleman would do, straightened up the see-through negligee that she was almost wearing.

Satisfied that the "lady" was safe and secure, he resumed his stroll down the aisle. Only this time, I noticed a little more spunk in his step and about an extra inch added to his stature. He had tangled with what he had feared the most and come out victorious. He also had held a beautiful model in his arms, if only for a moment, and helped her stand up on her own two feet. What man wouldn't feel proud!

Like the elderly gentleman avoiding the lingerie section, there are many things in my life that I try to avoid. In fact, I'll turn my head so far in the opposite direction, that I get a spiritual crick in my neck. But turning my head the other way never makes the problem disappear. As a matter of fact, when I try to ignore a problem or situation that I need to deal with, I usually end up running smack-dab into it, and it falls directly into my lap. Then like the elderly gentleman, I am forced to look the problem squarely in the face. It would be so much easier to deal with a situation while I'm still standing on my feet than to wait until I'm sprawled out on the floor with disaster lying in my arms.

What are you avoiding today? What fears do you need to face? Blinders aren't the answer. Instead, put your trust in God. Proverbs 3:5-6 says, "Trust in the LORD with all your heart, and do not lean on your own understanding. In all your ways acknowledge Him, and He will make your paths straight." Sometimes that path may lead you directly into what you fear the most, but after the Lord has seen you through the crisis, you'll probably notice an extra spring in your step and the courage to move on.

Swollen Imaginations

Fear can be a paralyzing force that prevents us from moving forward with our lives. Yet many times what we fear is not even reality but only speculation. For example, take the case of one of my husband's patients, Ada.

Ada had an uneventful dental visit with my husband—just a routine filling. So he was a little surprised when she called him at home the night after her appointment. "Dr. Jaynes," she groaned, "I'm having severe pain and swelling right beside the tooth with the new filling. It's killing me, and I can barely open my mouth."

"Well Ada," he answered, "I can't imagine what the problem could be. I'll call you in a prescription for some pain medication, and you come by the office first thing in the morning and let me take a look."

I was Steve's humble assistant in the office that week and was amazed at Ada's appearance when I saw her in the waiting room the next morning. Her eyes were half closed, and she could hardly walk as I led her slowly back to his treatment room. There did appear to be a slight swelling in her upper-right cheek.

Ada sat down in the chair as if every move took much effort. She could barely open her mouth to let Steve see what the problem might be. Finally, she did manage to open it slightly. Steve peeked inside, gently lifting her lip, and a huge grin spread across his face. He reached in and removed a small cotton roll from the area between her cheek and tooth.

Ada's eyes popped open, as she miraculously bolted upright in the chair. "What did you do?" she asked, all signs of weakness gone.

With a smile, Steve held up the small piece of cotton. "This is what was causing you so much 'pain.'"

Of course, Ada was terribly embarrassed and wanted to crawl under the chair. The day before, Steve had placed a cotton roll between Ada's cheek and tooth to keep the area dry while he placed the filling. I, his now more humble assistant, had forgotten to remove the cotton when he had finished. When the numbness wore off, Ada had felt her swollen cheek and thought the worst. As the night wore on, she had worked herself into a frenzy and could barely raise her head from the "pseudo" pain she had imagined. Never once did she open her mouth and look inside. Of course if she had, what she would have seen was just a little piece of harmless white cotton.

I had to stop and think, *Lord, do I have any cotton rolls in my life that need to be removed? Are there any little harmless worries that I have tucked away, that I have made into colossal problems?* I felt certain that some of the problems that keep me from moving forward at times are in reality just as harmless as that piece of cotton.

Sometimes, little comments that others have left behind fester and grow in my mind until they become seemingly insurmountable problems. But I know that if I just open wide and let God shine His light and look inside my heart, I might be surprised to find something harmless. Also, I know that if I don't have the courage (or the common sense) to look myself, the Doctor will be more than happy to remove it for me.

Ada had come into the office that day full of fear and false pain. But she left with one less cotton roll and a lesson: When we are feeling really "down in the mouth," we need to take a look inside ourselves and examine whether our problem is real or imagined.

The Bride in the Box

"Here comes the bride, all dressed in white." Every little girl dreams of the day when she will become a beautiful bride. At four years old, I was no exception. It wasn't the dream of becoming a wife that captured my imagination but merely the dream of the wedding day itself.

I had visions of gliding down the red-carpeted aisle of my hometown church, adorned in a flowing white satin and chiffon wedding gown, studded with a million tiny pearls. My twelve-foot lace veil would fill the aisle from side to side just like Julie Andrew's in *The Sound of Music,* and on my feet would be tiny satin sippers. I would carry a large bouquet of white roses mingled with a spray of delicate baby's breath.

Who the groom would be was of little consequence. This was clearly to be my show. On rainy days, I would wrap a sheet around my head and practice the wedding march down the long hallway of my parents' home.

Apparently, one of my uncles understood the secret longings of four-year-old girls and presented me with a two-foot-tall doll dressed in full bridal regalia. This was clearly the most beautiful doll I had ever seen. Along with her white wedding gown and veil, she had short-cropped, curly-brown hair that felt as real as my own; soft, plump, pink skin, and movable eyelids lined with thick black lashes. Her eyes opened and closed with her changing positions so that when she lay down in her box, she resembled Sleeping Beauty. Her perfectly-shaped lips were small and dainty, and her crystal-blue eyes appeared strangely real.

But there was one problem with this delightful gift. Because she was so expensive, my mother wouldn't allow me to play with her.

"You'll have to wait until you are older," she stated. "She's too nice of a doll, and you might tear her gown. We'll just keep her in the box until you're big enough to know how to take care of her."

The bride doll remained in her box, safely stowed away in the bottom drawer of my dresser. Day after day,

I would slowly open the drawer and stare at the doll as she lay sleeping inside the dark drawer like a treasure in a safety deposit box. Sometimes I would remove the box lid and gently stroke her soft pink skin, but I knew "woe is me" if I ever took her out of the box and played with her.

Now that I am an adult, my thoughts have gone back to that special gift. After a time, I forgot about the bride in the dresser drawer, and today, I don't even remember what became of her. As a child, my relationship with the Lord was much like my relationship with the doll. God was Someone to be revered and feared, but certainly not Someone to be touched and enjoyed. I had the impression that God, like the doll, was also to be kept in a box: a big brick building with a large steeple on top, that was only to be opened on Sunday and special holidays. But He was certainly not Someone who could actually abide in your home or live in your heart.

The Shorter Catechism, written by the Westminster Assembly in 1647, states, "The chief end of man is to glorify God and enjoy Him forever." Enjoy Him! That was such a revelation to me when I heard it for the first time. It took me years to understand what it meant and how to go about the business of enjoying my Heavenly Father. But David understood how to enjoy the Lord.

He wrote, "In Your presence is fullness of joy; in Thy right hand there are pleasures forever" (Psalm 16:11). I suspect David knew how to "have a good time" with the Father.

Not only did I have to learn what it meant to enjoy the Lord, but I've moved on to learn how to enjoy His gifts as well. 1 Timothy 6:17 says that God richly supplies us with all things to enjoy. Webster defines "enjoy" as "to take pleasure or delight in, to have the use, the benefit or advantage of." Even though the bride doll was a precious gift to me, I did not have the use of her as a toy, the benefit of holding her, or the advantage of hours of creative play. Likewise, if I keep the many gifts the Lord has given me in a box with the lid tightly shut, they serve no purpose, and I receive no benefit in having them.

No longer will I keep God or His gifts in a box for safekeeping. I will sing with Him, talk with Him, take walks with Him, and yes, even dance with Him. And I don't have to wait until I am big enough to take care of Him, because He is big enough to take care of me.

Rearview Driving

I've made an incredible discovery over the past few decades. It is hard to move forward when you spend your time looking backward. That's true in driving as well as in life.

One day, I sat in my car, dreading the drive down my friend Brenda's driveway. No, it wasn't a descent from a towering mountain, but backing out of Brenda's mountainous driveway had me hesitating at the wheel. The concrete path resembled a ski slope, and I was parked at the top, the nose of my car pointing heavenward and the rear slanting downward to the street below.

Normally, I would have rolled down my window and poked my head out to look where I was going. But that day, the clouds emptied their entire contents all at once, and I was dependent on my rearview mirror.

The driveway angled straight down, but as I looked into the mirror and inched my way backward, I found myself turning a little to the left, then a little to the right, and finally a little back to the left again. Twice, I bumped over the pavement onto the wet grass.

Why was it so difficult to back down this straight driveway? I had done it many times before. Then I realized that it wasn't the backing down that was the problem; it was backing down while looking in my rearview mirror. As I reached the bottom of the hill, it hit me. Is this why so many people have trouble staying on the road in their spiritual journeys? Are they driving through life looking in their rearview mirrors instead of straight ahead?

Paul says it well in Philippians 3:13-14: "Brethren, I do not regard myself as having laid hold of it yet (perfection); but one thing I do; forgetting what lies behind and reaching forward to what lies ahead, I press on toward the goal for the prize of the upward call of God in Christ Jesus."

Rearview mirrors serve one major purpose—to see what is behind you while moving forward. In my spiritual journey, it is essential to look back to see where I've been, how far the Lord has brought me, and what He has done in my life. In the Old Testament, leaders reminded their followers of God's mighty provisions and feats on their behalf. But it was done only as an encouragement to give them the strength and courage to press on. Unfortunately, I believe many people are looking back to place blame—not to move forward—and their lives are littered with "if onlys." "If only my father hadn't been an alcoholic." "If only I had been raised in a Christian home."

A warning is etched onto the glass of my mirror: "Objects in mirror are closer than they may appear." In other words, looking in the rearview mirror will distort your vision. It is hard to look at the past without changing the reality of the situation. People have a tendency to romanticize life and forget the negative, or they focus on traumatic situations and accentuate the negative.

So what's the answer? I do need to look back to see what the Lord has done for me and remind myself of His faithfulness. But I don't need to go through life looking backward to find someone to blame each time I veer off the road.

Rearview mirrors are helpful and necessary, but if we choose to drive through life looking backward instead of moving forward, we're in for a lot of wrecks.

Hot Head, Cold Feet

In my twenties, it seemed that all my friends were moving into the area of holy matrimony. A few weeks before my husband, Steve, and I were married, we attended the wedding of a high school friend of mine in a small Episcopal church. Because of the limited parking, we had to walk several blocks to get to the sanctuary. The July heat was hovering somewhere around one hundred degrees with at least a ninety-eight percent humidity. Needless to say, in coat and tie, Steve was rather hot by the time we reached our destination.

Because we didn't allow for the walking time, we were a few minutes late to the ceremony, and there was standing room only. We, along with several other latecomers, lined the walls like tin soldiers surrounding the pews. Much to Steve's delight, his spot was over an air-conditioning vent. The sweat was still pouring over his brow as the cool air from the vent filtered up his pant legs. But Steve's delight quickly turned into dismay when the room started closing in around him and swirling in circles. The sudden temperature change had been too drastic, and he knew that he was about to faint. He grabbed the pew in front of him and gently slid down onto a seat under a rather large lady, who was standing.

In a few moments after his body temperature regulated itself, he regained his composure and stood for the rest of the ceremony, nothing hurt but his pride. My friends had a great time teasing him, accusing him of fainting in fear when he thought about our wedding just three weeks away. He definitely gave a new meaning to the phrase "cold feet."

This episode made me think of the verse in Revelation 3:15-16 which reads, "I know your deeds, that you are neither cold nor hot; I wish that you were cold or hot. So because you are lukewarm, and neither hot nor cold, I will spit you out of My mouth." The Lord detests lukewarmness. But I suggest that He also detests it when Christians are both hot *and* cold at the same time. There are many who are on fire for God on Sundays but say their faith is "a private matter" during the rest of the week. As Steve's body proved, extreme hot and cold cannot coexist—something has to give.

Overheating—Again

I don't know much about cars, but I have learned a valuable lesson (actually the lesson was valued at about four thousand dollars). If you're driving a car, and that little red needle that fluctuates between "C" and "H" goes to the top and points to "H," you need to stop right away. Do not keep moving. Do not pass go. Do not collect two hundred dollars.

We once had a station wagon with a hot temper. So many things went wrong with that car, the repairman began to recognize my voice when I called the shop. First Corinthians 15:33 NIV says, "Bad company corrupts good character," and that car was definitely corrupting mine. It made me think evil thoughts and want to do bad things with a sledgehammer.

One day as I glanced down at the gauges, I noticed a needle pointing to a big "H" and assumed that meant the car was hot. Well, it was August, and frankly, I had been hot all day. So I figured, *What's the big deal?* In any case, I thought it would be a good idea to mosey on down to the dealership, ten miles away, and get them to check it out. Big mistake!

A few miles later, smoke started pouring out from under the hood. But did I stop? No, indeed! I just kept going, trying to make it to the repair shop before closing time. Finally, right in the middle of an intersection, the little engine that could decided that it couldn't any longer and died. Thus began my first lesson on just how important that little "H" was on my control panel.

"Mrs. Jaynes, you see that needle that is pointing to 'H'?" the repairman asked. "That means that the engine is runnin' hot. When you see that, you've got to stop right away. Since you kept goin', you burned up your engine. It's a goner. You'll have to get a new one."

"That sounds expensive," I moaned.

"Oh, it'll be about four thousand dollars," he answered, while continuing to poke around under the hood.

Four thousand dollars! And all because I didn't stop the car when it overheated . . . all because I didn't heed the warning signs.

Cars aren't the only things that overheat. I can think of more than a few times when I have overheated myself. There have been times when my coolant has leaked out all over the road or times when I have run out of the oil of gladness. There have been times when I've wanted to bite somebody's head off or set the record straight once and for all. Being stuck in traffic when I'm already fifteen minutes late to an appointment, having to go back to school because my son forgot a book in a subject that he has a test on the next day, and discovering that someone left a blue ink pen in his pocket that has gone through the washing machine, all make my engine overheat.

I saw an article in the newspaper once that read, "A man was coaxed out of his home in Issaquah, Washington, by police officers after he pulled a gun and shot several times at his personal computer, apparently in frustration." Ah, a kindred spirit.

My computer's safe from me pulling out an AK-47, because I don't own one. But my family, friends, and salespersons are not always safe from another lethal weapon—my tongue. James 3:8 says, "The tongue; it is a restless evil and full of deadly poison." I resemble that remark!

When I start to heat up, I have a tendency to stew a little bit, simmer, and mull over a perceived wrong. Ephesians 4:26 TLB reads, "If you are angry, don't sin by nursing your grudge." I'd lump stewing and nursing in the same category. Both should be a warning signal that the temperature needle is getting a little off center and too close to that big red "H." But before I blow a gasket and my coolant leaks out all over the road, I need to pull over and let my engine cool down.

One thing I did learn about this overheating business, which makes no sense to me, is that if your car is running hot, the best thing to do is turn the heater on. This lets the hot air escape and helps cool the engine. Maybe when I am overheating, instead of burning out my engine by continuing down the road, I need to learn how to have a Christ-like confrontation and let some of the heat vent. Maybe I need to write a psalm or two. David certainly was great at venting himself when he was overheated. I find myself reading the Psalms and saying, "Go ahead, David, tell God how you *really* feel."

Another course of action to temporarily treat a hot engine is to pour water in the radiator. Of course, you have to let the motor cool down a bit first or the water will immediately turn into steam. Many times in

Scripture, the Holy Spirit is referred to as the Living Water. If my temperature needle is leaning toward "H," maybe I need to read that as HELP HOLY SPIRIT! Spending time in prayer is a sure way to cool any engine down.

How about you? Do you know the warning signals that your engine is about to overheat? My suggestion is to pull off the road immediately and pray, "Help Holy Spirit!" Believe me, the price of driving with an overheated engine can be very costly and will make your moving forward process come to an abrupt halt.

Swine or Truth?

I read a bumper sticker once that said, "If mother's place is in the home, why am I always in the car?" Welcome to the new millennium where the car is indeed the moving extension of the home. Whether it's a mother running a carpool, a business woman sitting in commuter traffic, or a senior citizen volunteering in the community, the fact is, we live much of our lives in the car, which means God lives there with us and speaks to its mobile inhabitants. One such "moving" experience taught me about the importance of not jumping to conclusions.

John 8:32 is one of my favorite Bible verses. So much so, that I had a personalized license plate made that reads, JOHN 8:32. The verse says, "You will know the truth, and the truth will make you free."

My friend, Mary, noticed my license plate for the first time as we passed one day on the highway, and made a mental note to look up the verse when she arrived home. After she found the verse, she spent some time meditating and wondering why in the world I would put that verse on my license plate. She looked again to see if maybe there was some deep meaning that she was missing. Maybe it was a joke.

Mary gave me a call and asked, "What possessed you to put a Bible verse about pigs on your license plate?"

"What are you talking about, Mary?"

"You know. You have Luke 8:32 on your license plate."

The problem was, Mary had remembered the verse as Luke 8:32, not John 8:32. That verse reads, "Now there was a herd of many swine feeding there on the mountain; and the demons entreated Him to permit them to enter the swine. And He gave them permission." Can't you see it now, bumper stickers that read, "When pigs flew, Luke 8:32." Or a Chick-fil-A billboard with Luke 8:32 written in the bottom right-hand corner with the message, "Don't eat pork."

After I set Mary straight, telling her that she had the right verse but the wrong book, we had a good chuckle, but it was a "moving" experience for me. The next time I question someone's motives or actions, I need to remember that I usually don't have all the facts. I might have the right chapter and even the right verse, but I may be in the wrong book altogether. And that can make the difference between demon-possessed pigs and the spiritual freedom of the truth.

The Baby in the Nile

Imagine the ruler of the land has ordered a decree to kill all Hebrew baby boys under the age of two, and unfortunately, you are a pregnant Hebrew. That news would cause any mother-to-be to go into "prepartum" depression, and this was the situation in which Jochebed, the wife of Amram, found herself . But what a resourceful gal! After she gave birth to her baby boy, she hid him away in her hut and nursed him for three short months. Then when he was too big and too loud to keep under wraps, she made a little wicker basket, covered it with tar and pitch, and deposited her son in the bulrushes of the Nile River. The baby's older sister hung around, hiding in the background to see if anyone would notice her brother floating in his own personal ark and save his life.

As I traveled to the Christian Bookseller's Convention in Atlanta, Georgia, the Lord brought the story of baby Moses to my mind. For two years I had been in labor, working on a book of inspirational stories in hopes of one day having them published. My baby was now out of the womb. I had nursed it way past the age of weaning, and now it was too big and too loud to keep under wraps any longer.

Christian book publishers across the country were cutting back on accepting manuscripts, especially from unknown first-time writers like myself. Bookstore shelves were crowded with wonderful manuscripts from great authors. The Pharaoh had issued the edict: "There are too many books in the land. All unknown authors need to be hacked." But I was pregnant with book, and I had to save my "baby"!

"Lord," I prayed, "Why am I going to this convention? I am just a nobody, who wants to encourage everybody about the wonderful life they can have when they know a certain Somebody. But I am such a little fish in such a great big pond. I have already heard the edict from the Pharaohs of the publishing world. Should I quit? Should I turn around and go home?"

My answer from God was the story of baby Moses. In desperation, his mother had placed him in the Nile and hoped he would be rescued instead of destroyed. So that's what I did. I placed my baby in a nice little folder and said a prayer over its title page. The folder wasn't covered with tar, but you can be sure it was covered with a lot of "pitch." Then I placed the "baby" in the sea of acquisitions editors and stood by in the bulrushes to see if anyone would rescue the "baby" from doom.

Many of us have dreams of special tasks that the Lord has called us to do. It may be a dream to lead a Bible study group or start an orphanage or go back to school or write a book. As Florence Littauer says in her book, *Dare to Dream,* first we dare to dream and then we prepare the dream. But after years of preparing, these projects can become like our children. We hate to let go. But we can't keep them under wraps forever, any more than we can keep our children tied to our apron strings. There comes a time when the "baby" must be turned over to God. Then we wait . . . and hope . . . and pray.

Baby Moses was floating around in his little wicker basket when along came the Pharaoh's daughter to take a bath in the Nile. She saw Moses' boat, pulled him out, thought he was beautiful, and decided to keep him for herself. Then Moses' sister popped up from behind the bushes and said, "Hey, I know where you can get a great wet nurse for the baby." Moses' own mother had the privilege of nursing her son for two more years. Not only that, but she also was paid to do it!

I ended a busy day at the CBA convention with a prayer of gratitude and anticipation. "Thank you Lord for giving me this 'baby.' I now place it in your hands and place myself behind the bushes to wait." And I prayed that someone who resembled a Pharaoh's daughter would come along and think my "baby" was beautiful.

For all of us, a time comes to "place the baby in the Nile." It is difficult. It is heart wrenching. But it must be done. We must have the courage to move forward and take that step of faith. And hopefully, our "baby" won't have a face that only a mother could love.

Circles in the Sand

I've always heard that in our spiritual lives, we are either moving forward or going backward. But I think many of us are simply going in circles.

One night I was sitting on my sofa doing some paperwork when I noticed a large red fire ant crawling across my sand-colored carpet. Since I was comfortably molded into the seat cushion, I didn't want to get up. So I waited until the ant was within striking distance before I reached for my shoe to put an abrupt end to its journey. The carpet was just a few months old, and I didn't want Mr. Ant's remains to leave a permanent mark, so I just banged on him softly. Just in case he wasn't all the way dead, I left my shoe lying on top of him until I was ready to get up.

To my surprise, a few minutes later, a shaken ant eased his way out from underneath his leather prison and began to limp away. I guess his vision, equilibrium, or left side was impaired, because instead of making a mad dash toward the door, he tottered feebly, making a series of left turns and going in circles.

Thirty minutes later, my husband walked into the room. "There's a big ant crawling on the floor," Steve said.

"Yeah, I know," I nonchalantly replied.

"Why don't you get a tissue and get rid of him?" he asked.

"I will when I get up," I answered.

"Aren't you afraid he'll crawl away by that time?"

"Nope," I responded confidently. "He's been going around in circles for thirty minutes. I'll get rid of him when I get up."

Sure enough, forty minutes after the ant's trip to nowhere began, I finished my work, got a tissue, and sent him on a trip to visit the city's water treatment plant.

This scenario made me think about another creature who traveled in circles. Well, a lot of creatures—about two millions Israelites—and not for forty minutes but for forty years.

The Israelites had been under the Egyptians' shoe for four hundred years. Then God called Moses to convince Pharaoh that their brick-making days were over and it was time for them to move on. Moses was to lead this band of slaves to freedom—to a land flowing with milk and honey. With plagues that would excite any professional exterminator, God convinced Pharaoh that letting the Israelites go would be a good idea. He yelled, "Get those Israelites out of here!"

Because the Egyptians were so glad to see them go, they loaded up the Israelites with lots of gold and other valuable stuff. So they gathered up their belongings and left. Led by a pillar of fire by night and a cloud by day, they moved forward. After marching between the towering walls of the parted waters of the Red Sea, they sang for joy. "Hip-hip hooray! Now we're on our way!" Or so it seemed.

But they didn't joyously parade on to the land flowing with milk and honey. They didn't continue in reverence and awe of a God who had already performed more miracles in their presence than most people see in a thousand lifetimes. Instead, they started to grumble and complain, "We're sick of this food." They started to doubt God. "Did He bring us out here to die?" They started to question Moses' leadership. "What are we going to drink?" They bickered among themselves, argued with Moses, and disobeyed God. When it was time to march into the Promised Land, most of their spies said it couldn't be done. So each time they stiffened their necks, God told them to take a left turn.

For forty years, they wandered in circles in the sand, like the ant crawling in circles on my sand-colored carpet. An entire generation died out, and a new generation was born. One day, these new and improved Israelites came up with a plan. "Hey, we've got an idea," they reasoned. "Let's try obeying God and see where that leads us." It led them where obedience to God always leads—on a straight path to the Promised Land.

As I studied the Israelites' journey, I noticed a strange phenomenon. As long as they were going in circles in the desert, bickering among themselves, they didn't encounter many outside enemies. They only fought one battle.

But as soon as they crossed over the Jordan River, they were under attack from the left and right. And so it is with us today. Many of us have been led out of the slavery of Egypt (sin) and passed through the Red Sea (the atoning blood of Jesus) only to continue going in circles. Amazingly, in a circular walk, there are few battles. It's pretty safe—not much action. Satan doesn't need to spend his energy attacking this bunch, because they're absolutely no threat to him. But let them start walking in obedience and moving toward the Promised Land (a mature spiritual walk), and the battle's on.

Why didn't I get up from my comfy seat and dispose of the ant? Because I knew he wasn't going anywhere, so why bother. But if he had headed for the door, I'd have taken care of him immediately.

Are you facing enemies in your life—Gossip-ites, Mocker-ites, In-law-ites, Neighbor-ites? You must be headed in the right direction!

Dear Lord,

I don't want to be like the Israelites who wandered around in the desert, going in circles for forty years. My heart's desire is to hear Your voice in the burning bush of my life and obey Your bidding.

Forgive me when I dwell on the past, whether it's on my failures or successes. Forgive me when my passion and love for You grows tepid, and the living water that has been poured into me stagnates.

Lord, I let go of the things that keep me in a holding pattern, circling over the runway of life. Whether it's letting go of my fears, letting go of the past, or letting go of a much-loved project—anything that keeps me from spiritual maturity—I give it all to You.

Like the obedient second-generation Israelites, I step forward with anticipation, heading toward the Promised Land and singing a song of someone who's finally moving on!

Amen.

Elise
2000

The Stairs

Moving Up

Imagine you have just been informed that you have inherited a multi-level mansion equipped with every conceivable treasure. You run up the curving brick sidewalk, throw open the massive oak doors, and excitedly run from room to room, hardly believing the good fortune bequeathed to you! However, what you discover are not the surroundings fit for royalty that you expected, but rather sensible chambers, adequately furnished and sparsely decorated.

In the foyer, a beautifully carved, winding staircase, adorned with plush crimson carpet, beckons you to climb to the next level. You consider the steps, look back over your shoulder and decide, "Hey, the lower level's enough for me. Besides, I'm afraid of heights. I'll just stay down here where it's safe."

Unbeknownst to you, the upper levels house all your inherited treasures, and you've chosen to stay in the servants' quarters. Upstairs await a gilded ballroom, a dining hall with crystal chandeliers, four-poster beds with down-filled mattresses, a safe filled with enough gold and silver to last a lifetime, and jewelry boxes brimming with family heirlooms.

All that stands between you and these treasures is the staircase. What keeps you on ground level? Contentment with mediocrity? Lack of knowledge? A fear of the unknown?

We all have an inheritance from our Heavenly Father. We have been blessed with every spiritual blessing. But oftentimes, we spend our days in the servants' quarters, never climbing the stairs to where the true riches are stored.

Approach the stairs and climb—no run—to claim the spiritual treasures that are yours in Christ. Let's be children of God who are ascending, maturing, and moving up.

Grafted

Julianna came out of the womb ready to meet every challenge with determination, every celebration with enthusiasm, and every mystery with the passion of discovery. Her fiery-red hair was matched only by her fiery personality. She never did anything halfway; the throttle was always set on full-speed ahead. Of the Price's three children, Julianna was the one who spent the most time in the emergency room for stitches. She whirled through childhood, throwing caution to the wind.

One day, when she was twelve years old, Julianna rushed out the front door on her way to dance class. She slammed the door behind her, closing it before all of her fingers had cleared the doorjamb. Now you and I have probably slammed our fingers in the door a time

or two and remember wincing a bit. But Julianna never did anything halfway. She jerked to a sudden halt, spun around, and saw her appendages trapped in the closed door. When she opened the door to remove her hand, she was horrified to discover that she had amputated the upper third of her second-right finger.

"Help! Somebody help me! I've just cut off my finger!"

Fortunately, the woman picking her up for dance class was a nurse. She rushed to the screaming ballerina. "Julianna, where's your mom?" she asked.

"She's not here," Julianna answered between sobs. "Nobody's here but Daniel."

"Quick," the neighbor instructed, "Let's put some pressure on that nub. Daniel, come help us!" Daniel, Julianna's fifteen-year-old brother, ran down the stairs at the cry for help. "Julianna's cut her finger off. You have to find it. We've got to put it in some ice and take her to the hospital right away."

A pale-faced Daniel went to the scene of the accident. His stomach turned upside down when he saw their dog, Fletcher, licking his lips. But as Daniel hung his head, he saw the finger lying at his feet. Trying not to lose his lunch, Daniel picked up his sister's digit in a towel and handed it over to the nurse.

They made it to the hospital in time. The skilled doctor put Humpty-Dumpty back together again and told them to pray that the finger would reattach.

A few days later, Julianna unwrapped the bandages, afraid of what she might find underneath. What she saw was not a pretty picture. Instead of a finger, she saw a black mushroom-like thimble.

"Doctor, we took the bandage off today," Julianna's mom reported. "It's . . . it's black and crusty and looks like a mushroom cap."

"That's fine," he answered. "Don't worry. If nature is working properly, and it sounds like it is, the top will turn black, but underneath, nerves and blood vessels are reattaching. Underneath the thimble, a new finger is forming. In about three weeks, we'll know if the procedure worked. Just keep it wrapped and clean. We'll keep our fingers crossed."

Four weeks after this incident, I received a letter from my little red-headed friend. At the bottom she wrote, "P.S. Guess what? My crusty thimble fell off, and I have a new finger!"

Now don't ask me how this happened. It's a mystery to me. But Scripture tells of another grafting process that is just as miraculous. When God warned Adam and

Eve not to eat of the fruit of the knowledge of good and evil, He warned them that their punishment for disobedience would be death. They did eat, and immediately, their spirits died. Years later, their bodies died. As a result, every person after that was born with a dead spirit, including me. I was cut off from God.

But God demonstrated His love for me, that while I was still spiritually dead—cut off, dead, rotten to the core—Christ died for me and made it possible for me to be grafted into the living root, Himself. God has made me alive again through Christ.

Many days I act more like the old dead me than the new living me. But Ephesians 2:10 says that I am God's workmanship, and He is regenerating my heart and renewing my mind. One day that crusty old body will pass away, and I'll be standing before the Father with an incredible likeness to the One to whom I was grafted. Then I can write you a letter and say, "P.S. The graft worked!"

Time Traveler

My husband awoke one morning with a nostalgic urge to revisit the small North Carolina town where he spent the first eight years of his childhood. At family gatherings, he and his brother would recount endless stories of playing kick-the-can and baseball in their front yard, which was "at least the size of a football field." The long hardwood hallway in their spacious home, where they would slide sock-footed, was "at least as long as a bowling alley." They boasted of huge grassy hills, where they rolled their bodies from top to bottom, itching all the way.

So the little boy in Steve hopped on his horse—a gold Honda Accord—and rode off to look for buried treasure. With map in hand, he located the big "X" where those wonderful memories were made. He pulled up to the address, blinked in unbelief, and checked the map again. What he saw was not a spacious home, but a tiny square bungalow. The yard, "the size of a football field," was in reality the size of a baseball infield with the house sitting on the pitcher's mound. And the "rolling hills" were no more than two humps in the ground.

Steve spent the day, driving from one landmark to another, and each time, reality clashed with memory. He kept saying, "Everything is so small." This visit was a shocking blow to Steve's mental scrapbook, and part of him wished he had not gone back in time. The happy memories were still etched in his mind. But the hall was shorter, and the hills were smaller.

As I listened to my husband tell of his adventure, I wondered if this was how I would feel when I finally arrive at the home God has prepared for me in eternity. My world is so grand with majestic sunsets, an endless expanse of stars, and vast oceans. But one day, I'll go to a new home—a mansion with many rooms—where the streets are paved with gold. When that time comes, if I can return to earth for a day, I think my reaction will be the same as Steve's when he traveled back in time. "Wow, everything is so small!" It won't be because everything has shrunk, but because I will have grown.

The Winner

It was the first swim meet of the year for our newly formed, middle-school aquatics team. The atmosphere on the three-hour bus ride was electric with anticipation as the band of forty-eight adolescents thought of nothing but victory. However, the electricity turned into shock as our minnows filed off the bus and stared in disbelief at their muscle-clad, Neptune-like opponents.

Coach Huey checked the schedule. *Surely there's been a mistake,* he thought. But the schedule only confirmed that this was the right place and the right time.

The two teams formed a line on the side of the pool. Whistles blew, races began, and races were lost. Halfway through the meet, the coach realized that he had no participants for one of the events.

"Okay team, who wants to swim the five-hundred-yard freestyle?" the coach asked.

Several hands shot up, including Justin Rigsbee's. "I'll race, coach!"

The coach looked down at the freckle-faced youth and said, "Justin, this race is twenty lengths of the pool. I've only seen you swim eight."

"Oh, I can do it, coach. Let me try. What's twelve more laps?"

The coach reluctantly conceded. *After all,* he thought, *It's not the winning but the trying that builds character.*

The whistle blew, and the opponents torpedoed through the water and finished the race in a mere four minutes and fifty seconds. The winners gathered on the sidelines to socialize while our group struggled to finish. After four more long minutes, the last exhausted members of our team emerged from the water—the last except for Justin.

Justin stole breaths as his hands slapped against the water and pushed it aside to propel his thin body forward. It appeared that he would go under at any minute, yet something seemed to keep pushing him onward.

"Why doesn't the coach stop that child?" the parents whispered among themselves. "He looks like he's about to drown, and the race was won four minutes ago."

But what the parents did not realize was that the real race, the race of a boy becoming a man, was just beginning. The coach walked over to the young swimmer, knelt down, and quietly spoke. Relieved parents thought, *Oh, he's finally going to pull that boy out before he kills himself.*

But to their surprise, the coach rose from the concrete, stepped back from the pool's edge, and the young man continued to swim.

One teammate, inspired by his brave friend, went to the side of the pool and walked the lane as Justin pressed on. "Come on, Justin, you can do it! You can do it! Keep going! Don't give up!" He was joined by another, then another, until the entire team was walking the length of the pool, rooting for and encouraging their fellow swimmer to finish the race set before him.

The opposing team saw what was happening and joined the chant. The students' contagious chorus sent a chill through the room, and soon the once concerned parents were on their feet cheering, shouting, and praying. The room was pulsating with energy and excitement as teammates and opponents alike pumped courage into one small swimmer.

Twelve long minutes after the starting whistle had blown, an exhausted, but smiling, Justin Rigsbee swam his final lap and struggled to pull himself out of the pool. The crowd had applauded the first swimmer as he crossed the finish line, but they gave Justin the greater cheer for simply finishing the race.

In 2 Timothy 4:7 NIV, Paul writes, "I have fought the good fight, I have finished the race, I have kept the faith." I imagine when my race is over, there will be a cloud of witnesses cheering me on when I cross that finish line. Oh sure, my strokes may not have been as smooth as someone else's. I may not have sailed through my race as effortlessly as many who have gone before. But just the same, they'll cheer for me, for moving up and finishing the race.

The Right Credentials

Patsy Clairmont has been an inspiration to me ever since I first read her book, *God Uses Cracked Pots.* We were discussing my first book on the telephone one day and trying to set up a time to meet face-to-face when she came to speak at the Women of Faith Conference at the Coliseum in my hometown.

"Patsy, I'd love to spend some time with you before the conference, but I don't have a backstage pass. I won't have access to where you'll be," I explained.

"No problem," Patsy answered. "Just go to my book table and tell my son who you are. He'll bring you to me."

The day of the conference arrived, and I swam through a sea of women to reach Patsy's crowded book table. It wasn't hard to spot her son—a male version of Patsy herself.

After introducing ourselves, we were off to find his mom. First we passed through heavy mahogany double doors that led to an area called, The Crown Room, for the VIPs who attended professional basketball games. Then we hopped on an elevator that took us to an area where another group of VIPs (Very Inspiring People) were tucked away.

As I stepped into the elevator, a stern security guard pointed his accusatory finger in my face and pronounced, "You're not supposed to be here. Where's your backstage pass? You're going to be in a lot of trouble."

He whipped out his walkie-talkie and was not afraid to use it. Before I could force one word out of my dry mouth, Patsy's son stepped forward, showed the guard his credentials, and gallantly stated, "She's with me."

"That's right, mister," I agreed when I had once again found my tongue. "He's Patsy Clairmont's son, and I'm with him."

"Oh, okay then," the guard said, and he was off to seek and find other dangerous Christian women like myself who were attending the conference.

Upon exiting the elevator, I saw all of the conference speakers enjoying a few moments of refreshment and fellowship together. While they munched on their lunch, I was nourished with a few moments of Patsy's encouragement. The conference was an inspiring, uplifting experience, but perhaps the greatest lesson I learned took place on that elevator ride.

One day, we will all move into the spiritual realm to live with our Heavenly Father. As we make our way to His throne room and pass through heaven's doors, there may be someone lurking in the shadows, waiting to accuse us, to call us unworthy, and to question our credentials. In Revelation 12:10, Satan is called "the accuser of the brethren." I envision him standing in my path, pointing his crooked, gnarled, demonic finger in my face and saying, "You don't belong here! Where's your pass? What are your credentials?"

Then just as Patsy's son stepped forward to vouch for me, God's Son will step forward and say, "Leave her alone! She's with me. I'm all the credentials she needs."

And I'll reply, "That's right, mister. This is God's Son, and I'm with Him."

For all of us who are members of the family of God, we have free access into His presence to sit at His feet and feast at His banquet table. This is not because of our own merit but because of who He is and who we are in Him. In Christ, we have all the credentials we need.

The Interview

My palms were slightly sweaty, yet calm. My posture was poised, yet not stiff. My dress was conservative, yet fashionable. I waited in a small room lined with bookshelves, diplomas, and awards. A mammoth wooden desk dwarfed my small chair positioned in the center of the interrogation room.

It was my first job interview. After completing dental hygiene school and passing both state and national boards, I was ready to cross over the bridge to the land of the employed. Even though Dr. Ford, the man who would decide my professional destiny, seemed somewhat intimidating, I felt fairly confident. My grade point average was excellent and my board scores commendable. I was ready for anything this guy had to throw at me. I mused, *Let the games begin!* And so they did.

"What was the last book you read?" he asked.

"*Reviewing for National Boards* and *The Four Loves* by C. S. Lewis," I replied.

"What did you eat for breakfast this morning?" he questioned.

"Coffee cake and milk," I answered.

"What's your least favorite household job?"

"Dusting."

"What would you do if you bought a set of living room furniture and it went on sale the next day?"

"Return it and buy it back again at the sale price."

This line of rapid-fire questioning went on for forty-five minutes. For each question, I shot back an honest response. But all the while I was thinking, *What's this got to do with dentistry? Is this what I've studied so hard for?*

After a few more minutes of chitchat, Dr. Ford leaned forward, and with a sincere smile said, "Sharon, we would like for you to join our team."

I was shocked! In my naiveté, I looked my prospective boss in the eye and asked, "Aren't you even going to ask me what kind of grades I made in school?"

With that, Dr. Ford threw back his head and filled the room with thunderous laughter. With a twinkle in his eye, he answered, "I imagine they were pretty good."

I could feel the color start at the end of my toes and rise to the top of my head. How did that comment escape my practiced lips? How could I say such a thing? I wanted to crawl under my chair and never come out.

Thus began my career in dentistry. I learned a lot over the next few years, but perhaps one of the most important lessons took place in the interview. What I discovered was that Dr. Ford was much more interested in my character than my scholastic accolades. Even though the questions seemed pointless to me, they spoke volumes about my life choices in common everyday situations.

I imagine my final interview with the Boss of the universe will have many such similarities, because He also is more concerned with my character than my performance, my heart than my achievements, and my compassion than my sacrifice. For that last interview, God will ask each perspective applicant, "Do you confess with your mouth Jesus as Lord and believe in your heart that I raised Him from the dead?"

"Yes, I do."

"Then come on in," He will reply. "We'd like to have you join our team."

"But wait a minute!" many will reply. "Aren't you even going to ask about my marks down there on earth? What about my ribbons and trophies?"

And the God of the universe will throw back His head and fill the heavens with thunderous laughter.

Messenger from Heaven

My new friend, Katie, lay in her bed, trying not to think about the pain in her abdomen. For years, she had nursed the sick back to health. But now, she was the patient. Just four weeks had passed since her doctor had uttered the words that kept echoing in her mind.

"Katie, it isn't an ulcer, like we originally thought. It's cancer—pancreatic cancer. It has already spread to your liver and your lungs."

"How long do I have?" she questioned.

"I'd say about three to six months."

Three to six months! She replayed her past fifty years on the stage of her mind. Her thoughts were filled with frantic questions: *How did this happen? What went wrong? How did I get to this point?*

Katie had accepted Jesus as her Savior when she was a young child. But that seemed like a lifetime ago, and in a way, it was. Now her thoughts were filled with shame, regret, and guilt. The verses about the Samaritan woman at the well came to mind. Jesus spoke to the woman and said, "Go call your husband and come here" (John 4:16).

She answered, "I have no husband" (verse 17).

Jesus replied, "You have correctly said, 'I have no husband'; for you have had five husbands, and the one whom you now have is not your husband" (verses 17-18).

"Lord, you know all that I've done," Katie prayed. "How I've fallen away from following You! I've been married twice, and the man I'm living with now is not my husband. Is that why this is happening to me? Am I being punished? People have told me that You still love me, but I feel so alone. Have you left me, too, like all the other men in my life?"

Katie reached for her Bible, and it fell open to Luke 3:22 where John was baptizing Jesus. "And the Holy Spirit descended upon Him in bodily form like a dove, and a voice came out of heaven, 'You are My beloved Son, in You I am well-pleased.'"

Tears ran down Katie's dry cheeks like streams in the desert. "Where are you Lord? Please don't desert me."

Katie turned her head to look out at the sun glistening over the tranquil lake in her backyard. Suddenly, as though he emerged from the pages of Luke 3, a dove fluttered to her window sill and perched on its ledge.

Katie hugged her Bible to her chest as she locked eyes with the dove. He seemed to say, "Yes, Katie. I do love you. You may have strayed away from the path that I had marked out for you, but that hasn't changed My love. I never left you, and I'll stay right here by your side until the day I come to take you home."

The dove stayed on the windowsill for quite some time, and Katie thanked God for sending His messenger like the one from long ago. Indescribable warmth penetrated Katie's body as she realized that God did, indeed, still love her.

Three months later, that dove came again to my friend, Katie. Only this time, when He soared back toward heaven, Katie's spirit went with him.

Inducted

"Sharon? This is Mary Ruth. I am so excited! Let me read you this letter that Alex just received from his school today."

"It says, 'Dear Alexander, We are pleased to inform you that because of your high grade-point average and excellent exhibition of character, you have been inducted into the National Honor Society.' Isn't that great!" the proud mother exclaimed.

Mary Ruth was so excited when she got this important letter in the mail and couldn't wait to read it to me over the phone. We rejoiced together over Alex's accomplishment.

But three months later, she called me back with a different letter. "Sharon, this is Mary Ruth. You won't

believe what I got in the mail today. We got another letter from school, and it reads 'Dear Alexander, We are sorry to inform you that because your grade-point average has fallen below the necessary requirements, you are no longer eligible for the National Honor Society."

In other words, Alex was *inducted,* but then he got *deducted.* This is not the kind of letter a parent wants to open. However, it made me think about how glad I am that since I have been inducted into the family of God, I never have to worry about the possibility of being deducted because I haven't kept up my spiritual grade-point average. Ephesians 2:8-9 says, "For by grace you have been saved through faith; and that not of yourselves, it is the gift of God; not as a result of works, so that no one may boast."

I have not been initiated into the kingdom of God because of anything I've done. It is a gift. It's a good thing, too, because I could never make my grades good enough to get in, and I could never maintain the grades to stay eligible. The good news is Jesus has already done it for me. He took the test. He passed with flying colors, and I reap the benefits.

I imagine a letter like this one coming to my house: "Dear Sharon, Congratulations! Because of the shed blood of Jesus Christ, His call on your life, and your submissive heart, you have been inducted into the Heavenly Honor Society. All the requirements have been met once and for all. Signed with love, Jehovah."

The Guest Book

Just before leaving our rented condominium after a week of sun, sand, and surf at Hilton Head Island, South Carolina, we found a treasure tucked under some old magazines on the coffee table. It was a six- by eight-inch white guest book signed by previous vacationers who had also shared a relaxing week away from home.

Feeling somewhat like a "peeping Tom" craning to peer into someone's window, we cracked open the book and stole a glimpse into the personalities of our fellow travelers. With each entry, we visualized what the guests looked like, decided if we would like to invite them over for dinner, and surmised whether they had had an enjoyable vacation together.

Have a look for yourself and decide with whom you would like to share a cup of coffee or have as your neighbor:

- "Thank you very much for the use of your condo. We thoroughly enjoyed our first, but not last visit to S. C." Mr. and Mrs. J.D.
- "Had a great time. Enjoyed your villa very much! However, you need to have the springs in the couch repaired. Very uncomfortable to sit in. Thank you." Mr. and Mrs. E.C.
- "We have decided that this is where we'd love to live. It's a golfer's dream. Your courses are beautiful. The girls loved the beach, parasailing, bike rides, horseback riding, shopping! I love my tan. We will be back to visit! If you are ever in Arkansas, come to Stuttgart. We are 50 miles east of Little Rock. Stuttgart hosts the World Championship Duck Calling Contest every year during Thanksgiving weekend. We are known as the "Rice and Duck Capital of the World." Riceland Rice comes from our little town and the ducks feed off of the rice fields during the winter after harvest. It is some of the best duck hunting anywhere. Thank you for the use of your condo. We've had a great week here." M.L.

- "We really enjoyed your villa, but we won't be staying here again. We just booked another villa at Colonnade for next year a couple of doors down for almost $300 less." Mr. S. and H. T.
- "Hello. My name is A. and I got here yesterday. So far we are having a good time. I'm eleven years old and I came here with my mother, grandmother, and my Aunt L. She got here at the same time we did, but she is leaving tomorrow. We came all the way from Lake Wylie, S. C. I love it here and might be back next year."
- "It has been a fabulous time. This villa is bigger than our home! My niece is sure she saw a whale at the Old Oyster Factory, but we are sure she saw a buoy. G. and Dad played golf together and we all played mini-golf. We went bike riding and 'gator chasing.' The ocean is breathtaking. I've never seen it before, so I'm still in awe! I love the wildlife and my turtle friend says, 'Hi!' B. and C. M.
- "We were very impressed with the condo. It was the best vacation we ever had." W. and D. A.
- "When we first came, the keys wouldn't fit, you forgot to give us a pass, and we almost ran over a biker. Get better service! Two grandmas were with us! Sixth time here—never happened before." S.S.

Pretty revealing, wouldn't you say? As we rated each guest from one to ten, I thought about the entries I have written with my daily life. In the New International Version of 1 Chronicles 29:15, it calls us "aliens." We are "sojourners and tenants" in the New American Standard version. That doesn't mean that we are little green men from Mars. But it does mean that we are guests while on this earth. Our real home is in heaven.

What entries am I writing with my attitudes, actions, and words for all the world to see? Will they think that I was a crabby old lady who wanted better service? Will they think I savored each day here with my wonderful family? Will they think that I would have preferred another life just a few doors down? Or will they think that I so enjoyed my time here that I wanted to share it with anyone and everyone who was passing through?

I've always heard the phrase, "My life is an open book." In this case, it certainly was.

Know what we wrote in the guest book? "Thank you for the use of your beach home. July fourth is a time to celebrate our great country with its many freedoms. Our hope for all who follow us here is that you will know the freedom which comes from knowing the Truth (John 8:32)." Steve, Sharon, and Steven Jaynes

Paul's Return

From the time our golden retriever, Ginger, was a pup, she has contracted ear infections and had trouble with dry itchy skin, both of which have to be treated with antibiotics. One particular day, Ginger's sensitive skin was causing her discomfort. She was scratching as much as she was breathing, so I decided to make a trip to the veterinarian's office for some medication. The office was unusually busy on this summer day, and the line at the checkout counter was five customers deep. I was the caboose.

One lady at the front of the line held a mountain lion of a cat who had everyone's undivided attention. The entire waiting room stared wide-eyed as this woman carried on a conversation with her feline.

"Fluffy," she scolded, "You were a naughty boy when you ran out in the street on Monday and sat on that yellow line." Then she cocked her head as if listening and continued, "Oh, was it Tuesday?" She acted as if the cat had heard, understood, and corrected her. This conversation went on for several minutes. Occasionally, the cat would look up at its master with that bored Garfield look that clearly said, "Lady, you're cuckoo."

Then she turned to the onlookers behind her to explain. "Fluffy is the reincarnation of a deceased friend of mine. My good friend, Paul, passed away not too long ago. Then two days later, Fluffy appeared on my doorstep out of nowhere; and he has been with me ever since." She was convinced that Fluffy was, indeed, Paul revisited. Poor Fluffy. Poor Paul. Poor lady!

At this explanation of Fluffy's heritage, for once in my life, I was glad to be at the back of the line. It was embarrassing. I was embarrassed for her and for Paul. The whole time she was conversing with Fluffy (alias Paul), he was giving his owner and the other humans in the room a look of disgust.

Then this woman started to encourage us fellow pet owners to join in the conversation with her feline. At that point, I decided that Ginger's skin problem wasn't so bad after all and that she could do without the

antibiotics for a few more days. I slowly inched my way back toward the door and bolted for the car.

Just so you know, when I'm gone from this world, don't be looking for me to return as a cow or a camel or, especially, a cat. I will have a new body, but it won't be covered in fur. In 1 Corinthians 15:42-43 AMP, Paul says that we will be raised immortal, imperishable, honorable, and clothed in glory. There are no hospitals where I'm going and definitely no veterinarian clinics.

An Easter Bride

It was a beautiful day for a wedding. The sun shone brightly, as the daffodils danced in the gentle breeze, nodding their happy faces in conversation. A choir of robins, cardinals, and finches sang rounds of cheerful melodies that floated through a clear blue sky, a reflection of the bride's sparkling eyes. The air had that crisp quality of spring, reminding us of the chill from winter's past and the warmth of the summer's promise.

It was Easter Sunday, 1997. In the Jewish custom of old, a man proposed to a young maiden and then promptly went away to prepare a home for his betrothed. When the young man's father gave his approval and agreed that the house was finally complete, the groom would then return and steal his bride away. The young maiden and her attendants would wait patiently with the oil lamps ever-burning in anticipation of his arrival.

Iris had been waiting for her husband to come and take her to the wonderful home that He had prepared for her. I believe her heart fluttered with the anticipation of seeing His face.

She wore a white dress with flecks of blue and carried a bouquet of pink carnations and white mums with a spray of asparagus fern as wispy as her baby-fine hair. A sweet smile spread across her face when she saw her beloved Jesus hold out His strong hand to help her across the threshold of this life into the halls of eternity. She walked into His loving embrace and drank in the loveliness of her surroundings that He had perfectly described in His many letters.

On that beautiful Easter Day, my husband's dear, sweet, seventy-four-year-old Aunt Iris went home to be with the Lord. As we all gathered around to say our last good-byes, I could not mourn. Sure I was going to miss her, but Iris had never been married on this side of eternity, and the vision I had in my mind was of her joining the Lord as the bride of Christ. For me, it was not a funeral. It was a wedding.

Revelation 21:9 says that we, the church, are the bride of Christ. In Matthew 25:1-13, Jesus describes a parable of how the bridegroom will come unexpectedly for His bride and take her home. May our lamps continue to burn brightly as each one of us joyfully anticipates His coming and take our final steps toward spending eternity with Him.

Dear Lord,

While You speak to me within the wall of my earthly home, help me keep a heavenly perspective and remember that this is not where I will spend eternity. My physical body is temporary, passing, and perishable, but we have a building from God, not made with human hands, that is eternal, ever-lasting, and endless (2 Corinthians 5:1).

With the anticipation of a bride as she makes preparations to be joined to her beloved, I expectantly watch for the day when You'll return for me. On that day, Your radiant face will light the skies, and I'll reach for Your hand, coaxing me to a new place where I'll be moving up.

Amen.

Conclusion

I hope that as we have perused the rooms of my home you have felt the warmth of God's presence in the laughter and tears. But one day we'll enter our new home that the Master Builder has constructed for us. In Revelation 21, we catch a glimpse of what that heavenly abode will look like: walls of jasper and pure gold, a foundation of precious stones, gates made of a single pearl, and streets of pure gold like transparent glass. He will wipe away every tear from our eyes, and there will be no more dying or pain. There will be no need of the sun or moon, because the glory of the Lord will illuminate our lives both day and night.

But for now, while the Spirit of God dwells here with us like a precious treasure housed in vessels of clay, let's listen for His gentle knocking on the doors of our hearts. Let's feed on His Word and rejoice that He is our Sustenance for living. Let's bask in Christ's radiance and enjoy being surrounded by His love. Let's cease our striving and worship the One who gives rest for the weary. Let's sing praises to Him who has made us clean at last. Let's reach forward with the Holy Spirit who prompts us to keep moving on and anticipate the day when we will hear Him say, "Welcome Home."

While today God is at home in our homes, one day we will be . . . *At Home with God.*

About the Author

Sharon Jaynes is the president of The Proverbs 31 Ministry and cohost for the ministry's international radio segments. She also is a feature writer for their monthly newsletter, *The Proverbs 31 Woman,* and inspirational conference speaker for women's events from coast to coast. Sharon is the author of *Being a Great Mom—Raising Great Kids,* contributing author for *Stories for a Man's Heart* and *Stories for a Teen's Heart,* and *Chicken Soup for the Sports Fan's Soul,* and has written for various magazines such as *The Joyful Christian Woman, Decision,* and *Money Matters.* She lives in Charlotte, North Carolina, with her husband, Steve, and their son, Steven.

For information about The Proverbs 31 Ministry or to have Sharon speak at a women's event, please call toll free 1-877-P31-HOME, or write:

The Proverbs 31 Ministry
P.O. Box 17155
Charlotte, NC 28227

Additional copies of this book are available
from your local bookstore.

If you have enjoyed this book, or if it has
impacted your life, we would like to hear from you.
Please contact us at:

RiverOak Publishing
Department E
P.O. Box 700143
Tulsa, Oklahoma 74170-0143